Also by Patrick Lencioni

Leadership Fables
The Five Temptations of a CEO
The Four Obsessions of an Extraordinary Executive
The Five Dysfunctions of a Team
Death by Meeting
Silos, Politics, and Turf Wars

Field Guide
Overcoming the Five Dysfunctions of a Team

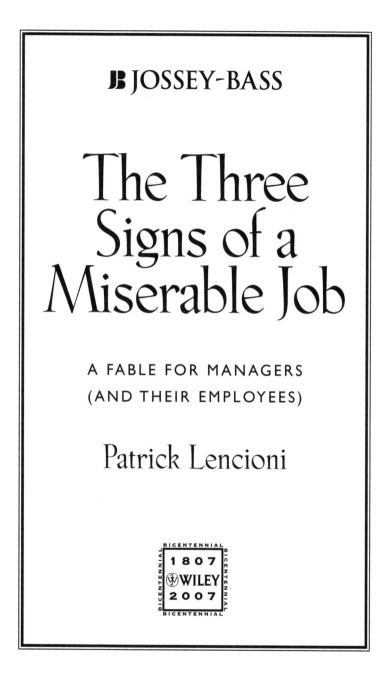

JB JOSSEY-BASS

The Three Signs of a Miserable Job

A FABLE FOR MANAGERS (AND THEIR EMPLOYEES)

Patrick Lencioni

BICENTENNIAL

1807

WILEY

2007

BICENTENNIAL

Published by Jossey-Bass
A Wiley Imprint
989 Market Street, San Francisco, CA 94103-1741 www.josseybass.com

Wiley Bicentennial logo: Richard J. Pacifico

Jossey-Bass books and products are available through most bookstores. To contact Jossey-Bass directly call our Customer Care Department within the U.S. at 800-956-7739, outside the U.S. at 317-572-3986, or fax 317-572-4002.

Jossey-Bass also publishes its books in a variety of electronic formats. Some content that appears in print may not be available in electronic books.

Library of Congress Cataloging-in-Publication Data

Lencioni, Patrick.
  The three signs of a miserable job : a fable for managers (and their employees) / Patrick Lencioni.
      p. cm.
    ISBN 978-0-7879-9531-7 (cloth)
    1. Job satisfaction. 2. Career development. 3. Employee motivation. I. Title.
    HF5549.5.J63L46 2007
    658.3'128—dc22

                                                        2007021305

Printed in the United States of America
FIRST EDITION
HB Printing   10 9 8 7 6 5 4 3 2

CONTENTS

For my sons, Michael, Casey, Connor, and Matthew.
May the jobs you have in life be purposeful and fulfilling.

INTRODUCTION

Work has always fascinated me, though I must admit, sometimes in a slightly morbid way.

I remember as a youngster being stunned and disturbed when I first learned that adults like my dad worked eight hours or more every day at their jobs. That was more time than I spent at school, and I could barely manage that!

And when I was told that many of those adults didn't really like their jobs, I was dumbfounded, unable to comprehend why people would spend so much time away from family and friends and not be happy about what they were doing. I suppose I also feared being in the same situation myself one day.

My fascination with jobs only grew when I too joined the workforce at the age of thirteen. As a summertime busboy at a large restaurant, I worked with waitresses and dishwashers and cooks and bartenders, most of whom were career employees. Later, during college, I spent my summers working as a bank teller, again with full-timers. In both of these jobs, I always found myself wondering whether my coworkers enjoyed their work, and over time I came to the inescapable conclusion that many of them did not.

Which continued to bother me.

My obsession with work reached a whole new level when I graduated from college and landed my first full-time job as a management consultant. That's when I learned about—and experienced for myself—something called the Sunday Blues.

The Sunday Blues are those awful feelings of dread and depression that many people get toward the end of their weekend as they contemplate going back to work the next day. I must admit that there were times toward the beginning of my career when the Sunday Blues began to take hold of me as early as Saturday night.

What was particularly troubling for me then was not just that I dreaded going to work, but that I felt like I should have enjoyed what I was doing. After all, I had landed one of the most sought-after, highest-paying jobs of anyone in my graduating class. I certainly wasn't in the kitchen of a restaurant shoveling other people's food into doggy bags, or standing alone in a bank vault counting cashier's checks. I was doing work that was interesting to me, and I was doing it in an upscale office with breathtaking views of the San Francisco Bay.

That's when I decided that the Sunday Blues just didn't make any sense.

You see, until then I had maintained a theory that eliminating dissatisfaction at work was all about finding the right job. A bad job was one that involved doing menial, boring work for low wages in an unattractive environment. And so I decided that the key to fulfillment was as simple as finding interesting work that paid well and kept me indoors. But even after having satisfied all those criteria, I was still miserable, which made me wonder if maybe I didn't really like consulting after all.

So I changed careers. And was no happier than I had been before.

My theory about job satisfaction was eroding quickly, especially as I met more and more people with supposedly great jobs who, like me, dreaded going to work. These were engineers and executives and teachers, highly educated people who carefully chose their careers based on their true passions and interests. And yet they were undoubtedly miserable.

The theory crumbled completely when I came across other people with less obviously attractive jobs who seemed to find fulfillment in their work—gardeners and waitresses and hotel housekeepers. And so it became apparent to me that there must be more to job fulfillment than I had thought. I wanted to figure out what it was so I could help put an end to the senseless tragedy of job misery, both for myself and for others.

And calling it a tragedy is not hyperbole.

Scores of people suffer—really suffer—every day as they trudge off from their families and friends to jobs that only make them more cynical, unhappy, and frustrated than they were when they left. Over time, this dull pain can erode the self-confidence and passion of even the strongest people, which in turn affects their spouses and children and friends in subtle but profound ways. Of course, in some cases the impact of job misery is not subtle at all; it leads to serious depression, drug and alcohol abuse, and even violence at work and at home.

Beyond the human misery caused by this phenomenon, the impact on organizations is undeniably huge. Though it may be difficult to quantify, the dissatisfaction of employees has a direct impact on productivity, turnover, and morale, all of which eventually hit a company's bottom line hard.

What makes all this so absurd is that there is indeed an effective remedy out there, one that is barely being used. It has no direct cost and can provide almost immediate benefits for employees, managers, and customers, thus giving companies who use it a powerful and unique competitive advantage.

But let me be very clear about something; the remedy I propose here is going to seem ridiculously simple and obvious at first glance. I am aware of that, and I must admit a little apprehensive about it. But when I consider how many managers fail to put these ideas into practice, and how many people continue to suffer through miserable jobs as a result, I come to the conclusion that perhaps simplicity and obviousness are exactly what is needed right now. In fact, I am convinced of it.

As the eighteenth-century author Samuel Johnson once wrote, "People need to be reminded more often than they need to be instructed." I sincerely hope that this little book is a simple and powerful reminder, one that helps you make someone's job—maybe your own—more fulfilling and rewarding.

The Three Signs of a Miserable Job

The Fable

SHOCK

Brian Bailey never saw it coming.

After seventeen years of serving as CEO of JMJ Fitness Machines, he could not have guessed that it could all be over, without warning, in just nineteen days. Nineteen days!

But over it was. And though he was better off financially than he had been at any time in his life, he suddenly felt as aimless as he had when he dropped out of college.

What he didn't know was that it was going to get a lot worse before it got better.

PART ONE

❖

The Manager

BRIAN

Early in his career, Brian Bailey came to an inescapable conclusion: he loved being a manager.

Every aspect of it fascinated him. Whether he was doing strategic planning and budgeting or counseling and performance appraisals, Brian felt like he had been created to manage. And as he experienced more and more success as a relatively young leader, he quickly came to the realization that his decision to forgo college made him no less qualified than his peers who had been to business school.

But then again, he hadn't had much choice about leaving school. Brian's family, being lower middle class to begin with, fell on particularly hard times when the Bailey walnut orchards in northern California were hit two years in a row by crippling frosts.

Being the oldest of five kids and the only one out of the house, Brian felt a sense of responsibility not to drain the family resources. Even with the financial aid programs offered at St. Mary's College, keeping him in school would have been a serious burden for the Baileys. And Brian's academic focus on theology and psychology didn't make the economic justification for staying in school any easier.

So, answering an ad in the newspaper, Brian took a line manager position in a Del Monte packing plant, and spent the next two years on a factory floor, ensuring that tomatoes and green beans and fruit cocktail were stuffed into cans as efficiently as possible. Brian liked to joke with his employees that he had always wanted to visit a "fruit cocktail farm."

As his father's orchard rebounded and the family's financial situation improved, Brian had a decision to make. He could go back to school and finish his degree—or continue to work at Del Monte, where he was on a fast-track to promotion and a possible shot at running his own plant one day. To the chagrin of his parents, he opted for neither.

Instead, Brian indulged his curiosity and took a job with the only automobile manufacturing plant in the San Francisco Bay Area. For the next fifteen years, he blissfully moved up various corporate ladders at the plant, spending equal time in manufacturing, finance, and operations.

Outside work, he married a woman he had briefly dated in high school, and who, ironically, attended St. Mary's after Brian had left. They moved to a small but growing community appropriately named Pleasanton, and raised a family of two boys and a little girl.

By the time Brian was thirty-five, he was vice president of manufacturing for the plant, working for a dynamic COO named Kathryn Petersen.

A few years after joining the plant, Kathryn had taken a personal interest in Brian because of his modest educational background, his work ethic, and his desire to learn. She kept Brian at one job or another in her part of the organization for as long as she could. But Kathryn knew it couldn't last forever.

THE BREAK

When a headhunter friend of Kathryn's called and asked if she would be interested in interviewing for the CEO position at a relatively small exercise equipment manufacturer in the central valley, she declined. But she insisted that her friend recommend Brian as a candidate for the job.

Looking at his résumé—and his lack of a college degree—the headhunter decided there was no way Brian would be hired, but—as a favor to Kathryn—agreed to let him interview. He was shocked when his client called two weeks later to say that Brian had been "the best candidate by far," and that he was being hired as CEO of JMJ Fitness Machines.

What impressed his interviewers at JMJ, and would continue to impress them on the job, was Brian's ability to communicate with and understand people at every part of the social spectrum. He seemed no more or less comfortable on the floor of the factory than he did in the boardroom, demonstrating a combination of competence and unpretentiousness that was rare among executives, even in the world of manufacturing.

As for Brian, he felt like a kid in a candy store, blessed to have the opportunity to do something he enjoyed. JMJ would benefit from that blessing.

JMJ

ocated in Manteca, California, a small bedroom and agricultural town sixty miles east of San Francisco, JMJ was a relatively young company that, for most of its first decade in existence, had merely survived. It did so largely by tapping into the relatively cheap labor in the area and mimicking its more innovative competitors. Though the company had managed to turn a modest profit, it was a minor player in a relatively fragmented industry, garnering less than 4 percent of the market and a position no higher than twelfth in terms of market share.

And then the company's founder and original CEO decided he'd had enough, prompting the call to the headhunter who ended up finding Brian.

The first year of Brian's tenure was no picnic as JMJ found itself enmeshed in a frivolous but distracting lawsuit. Ironically, that situation provided Brian with his first opportunity to prove himself as a leader, and provoke him to make some strategic changes.

For the next couple of years, Brian repositioned JMJ in every way possible. Most visibly to the outside world, he shifted the company's strategic focus almost exclusively toward institutional customers, which included hospitals, hotels, colleges, and health clubs.

Brian also injected a sense of inventiveness into the company by bringing in a few creative engineers and exercise physiologists from other industries. The net result of both these moves was a higher selling price for JMJ products, and unbelievably, higher demand for them too.

But as important as these changes were, nothing had a greater impact on JMJ's long-term success than what Brian did to its culture.

Like most other manufacturers in the area, the company had been plagued by relatively high turnover, low morale, and unpredictable productivity, living under the subtle but constant threat of unionization. Brian knew that turning around the organization would require him to change all that.

Over the course of just two years, Brian and his team managed to raise employee commitment and morale to unthinkably high levels, allowing the relatively obscure company in the central valley to establish a reputation for workforce satisfaction and retention. As a result, JMJ wound up winning more industry awards for being "A Great Place to Work" than it could cram into the glass trophy case in its lobby.

When reporters asked Brian for his secret to accomplishing this, he usually downplayed his role and told them that he simply treated people the way he would like to be treated. Which was mostly true, given that he had never really developed a specific methodology.

And as much as Brian publicly deflected credit for the cultural turnaround at his company, he quietly took great pride in the fact that he had given his people, especially the less privileged ones, more rewarding and fulfilling jobs than they would have found elsewhere in the area. More than any revenue goal or product innovation the company had achieved, this made Brian feel like his own job was meaningful.

Which is why selling the company would be so painful for him.

TREMORS

From a financial standpoint, JMJ was as solid as any medium-sized company could be. Under Brian's leadership, the firm had generated fifteen years of solid results, leapfrogging to become the number three—and at times, number two—player in the industry. With no debt, a well-respected brand, and plenty of cash in the bank, there was no reason to suspect that the privately held company was in any danger.

And then one day it happened.

It was a two-paragraph article in the *Wall Street Journal,* announcing that Nike was thinking about entering the market for exercise equipment. To most people reading the paper that day, the news was insignificant. For Brian, it was the precursor to an earthquake.

The chain reaction actually began two days later when Nike publicly identified the company it planned to acquire— FlexPro, JMJ's largest competitor. Before anyone knew what was happening, companies that had been operating independently for decades were positioning themselves to be swallowed up by brand name conglomerates from a variety of industries that were now interested in the exercise equipment market. For Brian and his 550 employees, it was only a matter of time.

CONSOLIDATION

ithin just a few days of reading that fateful article in the *Wall Street Journal,* Brian and his board numbly came to the conclusion that they would have to sell JMJ, and quickly.

As difficult as that might be, denial was not something Brian or his company could afford. After all, he didn't want to be the only company left standing when the music stopped—to find himself and his employees, all of whom owned stock, unrewarded for all their years of hard work. So he called one of his friends at an investment bank in San Francisco and asked him to help find a buyer for the company he loved.

Actually, Rick Simpson wasn't so much a friend as an old acquaintance. The two had lived for a year in the same suite in a dormitory at St. Mary's. Though never terribly close, they had managed to stay loosely connected ever since.

Brian had always found Rick to be brilliant and occasionally hilarious, as well as arrogant and insensitive. But for some reason, he could not bring himself to really dislike the man. As Brian explained to his puzzled wife, Rick always seemed to know when he was pushing the limits of obnoxiousness, and then recover by doing something genuinely redeeming.

In spite of his personality quirks, Rick had succeeded wildly in his career, developing a reputation as one of the best investment bankers in the country. In fact, he had become something of a celebrity in his field.

His response to Brian's initial call was typical. "So you've had enough of that cow town, huh?" Though that was certainly teasing, Brian was not in the mood for it.

"Well, I actually live in the Bay Area and commute over here. And I don't mind the valley so much. But I do need to sell the company."

"Why?"

"I don't have much of a choice. Nike just bought FlexPro, and if we try to compete against companies with that kind of marketing power, we're going to get crushed."

"Oh, right. I remember reading about that somewhere." Rick seemed to be rifling through some papers on his desk. "But aren't you're moving kind of fast?"

"Well, everyone's going to have to bail out eventually, and the smart ones usually go first."

"I can't argue with that," Rick agreed. "So you want me to help you find a buyer?"

"Yeah. And someone who sees our business as a strategic fit, and who understands our unique value."

"And what exactly is that value?" Rick wasn't being skeptical. He just needed to know.

"Well, our market share is nothing to sneeze at. Somewhere around 20 percent. We're a strong number two or three in a fairly fragmented market, depending on how you slice the pie."

Rick didn't respond, but Brian could tell he was writing it down, so he continued. "And we've got a solid balance sheet, a good brand name, strong sales projections for the next five quarters, and a few patents that won't expire for another couple of years."

"Sounds good so far. Is the market growing?"

Brian didn't hesitate. He knew the industry as well as anyone. "Projected at nine percent next year, though I think we'll come in somewhere closer to twelve."

"Sounds like you've done a hell of a job in that cow town."

Brian knew Rick well enough to appreciate the sarcastic compliment.

"We've done okay. Anyway, there's one more thing that I think a prospective buyer should know about us." He hesitated before continuing, not wanting to provoke another jibe. "We have the highest employee satisfaction in our industry. In fact, we're one of the best in any market. We've been named one of the top fifty medium-sized businesses to work for in America."

Rick didn't say a word at first, then chuckled. "Well, I'll have to adjust my valuation upward by a couple hundred dollars then."

"What's that supposed to mean?"

Brian's tone made it clear he was annoyed, so Rick backed off a little.

"I'm just teasing you, Brian. I'm sure you've worked very hard to build a nice culture over there, and I'll definitely put it in the package." He paused. "But I'm not going to lie to you. I don't think it'll translate into anything meaningful in terms of selling price."

"Well, it should." Brian knew he was sounding proud and defensive, but he couldn't help it.

As usual, Rick didn't mince his words. "It doesn't in my book. I mean, when I look at a company, I just want to know how fast the market's growing, how much of that market it owns, and whether it's in position to increase its share. I'm not big into the soft stuff. If it really matters, then it should be reflected in the bottom-line numbers anyway."

Nothing tweaked Brian more than being called soft, and he was tempted to slam the phone down right then and call someone else. But he knew that it wouldn't be in the best interest of his company. And somewhere in the darkest recesses of his brain, he feared that his cynical friend might be right.

So he took a breath. "You know, Rick, you can be a real jerk sometimes."

Rick laughed. "But you love me anyway, don't you, Brian? And you know what? I'll get you more money for your company than anyone else can."

Brian didn't respond, so Rick continued in a more conciliatory tone. "Hey, I don't want you to get the wrong idea. I'll admit that I've been following you and JMJ off and on for the past ten years or so. I have a pretty good idea about what you've done over there. In fact, I've even got one of your elliptical machines in my basement."

Brian silently accepted the muted apology. "Anyway, let me know later this week what you think we need to do."

"I'll call you Thursday. We'll do this right for you, buddy."

Brian said good-bye and hung up, amazed that Rick had not changed at all. And that he still couldn't hate the guy.

DONE

When Rick called on Thursday, Brian was expecting to hear that he'd made progress. After all, he was one of the best in the business. But Brian could not have guessed that Rick would have already identified a buyer and negotiated an informal ballpark selling price, one that exceeded anything he had imagined.

Rick's strategy was to exploit the "first mover advantage" card on both sides of the table, and he played it perfectly. He convinced the potential buyer to move quickly before other suitors could bid up the price. This made them a little more generous than they had intended to be. And he encouraged Brian to act before his other competitors entered the game, which would crowd the playing field and dilute his value on the open market.

So, after just a week and a half of conference calls, visits, and negotiation sessions, Brian signed the papers that gave control of his company to the country's largest medical equipment supplier. He would later admit that he was not at all prepared for the consequences of that signature.

BAND-AID REMOVAL

MJ's acquirer was not new to the acquisition game, and its executive team had adopted an extremely aggressive strategy when it came to integration. Their rationale was that it was better to accelerate a transition by moving quickly, even if that caused disruption, than to wait and let lethargy and fear take hold. "Like ripping off a Band-Aid in one fell swoop," their CEO explained before the ink on the contract was dry.

Their plan called for the name of the company to change immediately, which included everything from the way receptionists answered the phones to putting a new sign on the front of the building. It also meant that executives who weren't part of the company's long-term plans—which almost always included the CEO—were to be moved out as soon as possible. Brian's last day was set for just seven days after he had signed the company away.

Throughout the next week, Brian attended a number of emotional farewell luncheons and company celebrations marking the end of what had once been a humble little independent company. Though he deeply appreciated the overwhelming expressions of gratitude and affection from employees, especially the long-term factory workers whose lives had changed drastically during their time with the company, he found the experience to be so emotionally exhausting and overwhelming that he was quietly yearning for it to be over.

Finally, on a rainy Friday evening, after even the janitors had gone home, Brian packed his office and left the building for the last time. Preemptively wiping his eyes to keep any tears from escaping, he drove away wondering what the rest of his life would be like.

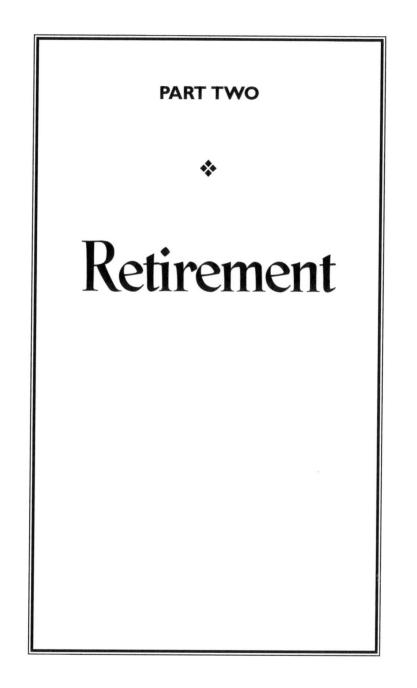

PART TWO

❖

Retirement

SABBATICAL

Leslie Bailey, Brian's wife of twenty-eight years, made him promise that he would get away from home for a week or two of complete rest before trying to come to terms with his retirement. They went to a little hotel in the Napa Valley.

For two and a half days she succeeded in keeping him from talking about his future, but he eventually wore her down. It happened while they were having dessert at their favorite Italian restaurant.

Brian was blunt. "I'm sorry, Leslie, but I can't wait anymore."

Leslie was confused. "For what?"

"To talk about work. What I'm going to do next."

Leslie laughed. "Oh. For a second I thought you were going to get frisky with me right here."

Brian responded with a straight face. "Well, that would be even better. You want to go out to the car?"

She laughed again. "Maybe later. For now, let's talk about work."

Brian paused. "I'm sorry. This was supposed to be a trip without—"

She interrupted him. "That's okay. I know you've been struggling since we came up here, and you've done your best. Spill it."

For the next two hours—until busboys politely kicked them out of the empty restaurant—the couple talked about Brian's state of mind, and his options. He was already restless. He wondered if his career had been a waste of time. Maybe he should dive right back into another company.

After a while it became clear that he and Leslie weren't on the same page. At times the discussion turned emotional, with Leslie doing most of the emoting.

"Listen, I haven't complained much over the past fifteen years. There have been plenty of late nights, and plenty of business trips and conference calls taken from home. And don't get me wrong. You've been a great father. But you did miss your fair share of recitals and ball games."

The comment seemed to provoke Brian, who responded in a calm but clearly frustrated way. "I don't think that's fair. I busted my butt to get to more of those events than most of the other dads. I don't think I should be sitting here feeling guilty for—"

Brian stopped when he saw that his wife was on the verge of crying.

"What's wrong?"

She took a moment to compose herself. "You're right. You shouldn't feel bad about that. You usually found a way to be there for the kids."

Brian felt a momentary sense of relief. Until she finished.

"It's really me that you weren't there for." And then the tears started flowing.

Now Brian felt horrible. Both because he knew she was right, and because she had never really complained about it until now. *How long has she been feeling this way?* he wondered.

It was at that moment that he vowed to become a better husband, to be more present for his wife. After twenty-eight years of work, Leslie certainly deserved it.

Besides, Brian had no real excuses now. With the sale of the company and the vesting of his stock, the Baileys suddenly had more money than they ever felt they needed. With no more tuition or braces to pay for, they could live a fairly comfortable lifestyle without Brian's ever having to work again.

And Leslie had no real need to work. After twenty years of being a turbo volunteer at school and church, and working full time as a teachers' aide for the past seven, she was more than ready for a change. As long as it involved her husband.

With their daughter in her last year of college and their boys gainfully employed in San Diego and Seattle, the Baileys were empty-nesters with no real restrictions or limitations.

"Okay," Brian said, grabbing her hand across the table, "for the next year or so, we can pretty much do whatever we want. The challenge is just to figure it out."

BRAINSTORM

For the next few days, Brian and Leslie went on long drives through the vineyards while they tossed around ideas for retirement.

Trying not to rule anything out immediately, the couple eventually discarded the notion of buying a boat or an RV or a biplane. As much as they had always enjoyed the outdoors, Leslie and Brian knew that they weren't really adventurers, the kind of people to live the life of nomads.

Leslie finally suggested that they find a nice little mountain home in the Lake Tahoe area where they could spend their winters skiing, and the rest of the year boating and golfing, activities they had enjoyed before having kids. She didn't have to do a lot of talking to convince Brian. He had been yearning to start skiing again for the past five years, and the thought of fishing and golfing during the off-season was certainly an attractive proposition.

"Let's do it," he announced with a smile on his face. "Who needs the rat race anyway?"

Soon enough Brian would come to realize that his honest answer to that question would have been *me*.

IMMERSION

For the next few weeks, the newly energized couple traveled back and forth to the mountains looking at houses, finally settling on a modest but modern log home at the southern end of Lake Tahoe, a few miles into Nevada. Two weeks later, over a month after "the Napa talk," as they came to refer to it, they moved in and began furnishing and decorating the new property.

Brian was more excited than he had expected to be, and enjoyed telling his kids and friends about the new cabin, with its view of the Heavenly Ski Resort slopes and the southern end of the lake. He even had his sales pitch down.

"Depending on what time of year you come up to visit, we can be skiing on the slopes, teeing off at a championship golf course, or dropping a line into Lake Tahoe within twelve minutes of walking out the door."

When an early snowstorm hit the area in November, Brian and Leslie excitedly began their first full season of skiing. It would be short and painful.

INJURED RESERVE

Brian was in better shape than the average fifty-three-year-old, which was not surprising given that he had run a fitness-related company for more than fifteen years. But no amount of time on an exercise bike or treadmill is adequate preparation for a sudden and drastic increase in skiing.

After three consecutive days on the slopes, Brian was ripe for a big fall. Though he was quickly regaining his form and confidence as a skier, he was also more fatigued and sore than he had been in years.

As he headed down on his last run of his fourth day, he was surprised to find the mountain virtually empty of fellow skiers. So Brian decided to have some fun. Venturing off the slushy grooves of the main run down to the lodge, he opted instead to take the deceptively icy slalom run used for local ski races.

By the time he was halfway down the hill, Brian's legs had started to burn and he found himself fighting to stay upright as he made his turns around the flags. Looking back on the situation, he realized that he should have simply veered off course and headed leisurely down the mountain. But being aware that the lodge was directly below and that at least a few people must have been drinking hot chocolate and observing his own private Olympic moment, Brian decided to go for broke.

As he approached the second to last flag, his right ski slid out from under him, setting off a chain reaction of imbalance followed by attempted recovery followed by a particularly unflattering spill. Before he knew what was happening, Brian was sliding headfirst down the mountain, with one ski, no poles, and a pair of goggles twisted vertically on his face.

More important, his knee was on fire.

CABIN FEVER

By the time the doctors were done with him, Brian left the community hospital on crutches, initially relieved by their assurances that he was lucky not to have done major damage that would require surgery. But when they told him that he'd be laid up for several weeks and that his ski season was over, he started to worry.

It wasn't just that Brian would miss skiing—though he certainly would—or that he would have nothing to do. The physical rest actually sounded pretty good to him, and he owned a stack of books that he had been meaning to read for years. It was the idle time he dreaded most, because he knew that it would tempt him to start thinking about work again.

For the first two weeks, Brian did his best to keep himself entertained and content.

Leslie's presence was his saving grace. The couple could spend more time talking, watching movies, and just being together than they had since their first son was born.

But eventually, Brian found himself fighting off a mild case of depression. He initially attributed it to the lack of physical activity. Though he was no triathlete, Brian had grown accustomed to some kind of regular exercise, and for the first time in his life he was unable to work out at all for an extended period of time.

And then there was the weather. One of the heaviest early snow seasons in the last fifty years had kept the immobile former executive homebound. Over the course of one five-day period, he couldn't go outside for more than fifteen minutes at a time.

But Brian eventually came to the ironic conclusion that his biggest problem was his need for a problem. He yearned for a business challenge to figure out.

Of course, he knew that Leslie would never stand for a sudden retreat to the Bay Area and corporate America, and rightly so. Brian couldn't even hint at such a move. Still, he had to find something real to do because, until he did, he would go stir crazy like a prisoner. And though his living quarters certainly didn't look like a penitentiary, as Brian liked to remind Leslie, "A jail is still a jail even if it has satellite TV and a picture window overlooking Lake Tahoe."

FURLOUGH

On his first day without crutches, the weather miraculously seemed to break, so Brian and Leslie took advantage and went for a long drive. As they were well into the second half of the loop around the lake, the couple decided to pick up food for dinner on the way home, and as usual, Leslie won the debate over what to order. She opted for Italian—a decision she soon regretted.

They decided on Gene and Joe's, a downscale Italian place a few blocks off the highway near their cabin. Leslie called ahead so that the food would be ready for them.

Brian and Leslie had never actually been to the restaurant, though they had ordered pizza or pasta for delivery on a few occasions during Brian's recent recuperation. It appeared to be open during late afternoons and evenings only.

The building itself was white stucco, with a Spanish-looking tile roof. Painted grapevines and Italian flags adorned most of the exterior, giving it a dated if not slightly tacky look. But the food was pretty good, and Brian and Leslie had always preferred unpretentious restaurants with big portions to overly sophisticated ones that sent you away hungry.

As they pulled their '93 Explorer into the parking lot, they noticed a drive-thru pickup window on the side of the building, something neither of them had ever seen at an Italian restaurant. They decided to give it a try.

After sitting at the window for a moment, it became apparent to Brian that no one was ready to help them. Peering into the restaurant through the window, he noticed that there was almost no one inside. Brian and Leslie agreed that it was too early for the dinner crowd, and that the place would probably be packed later in the evening when hungry skiers were driving home after a day on the slopes.

"This kind of reminds me of my first summer job during high school." The tone of Brian's voice indicated equal parts nostalgia and lament.

"Mr. Hamburger?"

Brian corrected her. "That would be Captain Hamburger."

"What a dive that place was."

"Yeah, but somehow we managed to have a ball working there."

"Didn't you get robbed once?"

"Twice. Which is why I quit and took a job on the graveyard shift at a potato chip plant. Which might sound bad, but in reality was even worse."

Leslie chuckled at the familiar joke.

Brian went on. "That was one long, miserable summer."

"But it turned out to be a good thing."

Brian frowned, and his wife explained.

"It made you get that job waiting tables at Carrows, which was the best job you ever had because that's where you met me."

Brian thought about it for a moment. "No, I'm pretty sure Captain Hamburger was better."

As Leslie punched her husband in the arm, their trip down memory lane was interrupted by someone finally coming to the window.

Brian was surprised to see that it wasn't a kid but rather a man in his mid-forties. He had a wedding ring on his finger and a tattoo on his arm, and was wearing a T-shirt with a picture of two smiling bald men Brian decided must be Gene and Joe. Across the shirt in alternating green and red letters was "Pizza and Pasta. Here, There, Everywhere."

What's a married, middle-aged guy doing working at a place like this? Brian couldn't help but wonder.

"Can I help you?" the man said without emotion.

"Yeah, we called in an order. For Leslie."

Without saying a word, the man retreated into the building, and returned a few moments later with a bag and a small pizza box. "That'll be fifteen eighty."

Taking the food in through the window, Brian handed the guy a twenty-dollar bill. "You can keep the change."

"Thanks." The response seemed only mildly grateful.

Four minutes later the retired couple arrived at their cabin and began removing their food from the bags, when Leslie let out a moan.

"Dang it. They forgot my salad again."

Brian took a breath. "I'll go get it."

"Oh, don't worry about it. It's not that big a deal." She wasn't convincing.

"No, it's the second time they've done this. It'll take me ten minutes."

GOING IN

When Brian arrived at the restaurant, he decided to get out of the car and go inside.

With the exception of one table with two older customers in the corner eating a very early dinner, the room was empty. Brian walked up to the order counter, where he waited for someone to help him. No one.

A quick survey of the area behind the counter made it clear that Gene and Joe's was a tired place as well as a lonely one. The cash register must have been twenty-five years old. The carpet was worn in the high-traffic areas and frayed around the edges. And a handwritten sign taped to the counter read: *help wanted—cook, delivery driver, weakend manager.* Brian smiled at the misspelling.

What might have once been a vibrant little restaurant was now merely surviving, Brian decided, and probably only because of its convenient location near the highway.

Finally, a young Hispanic employee appeared. "Can I help you?" He greeted Brian with a tone that was a little more enthusiastic than the drive-thru guy.

"Uh, yeah. I just picked up some food in the drive-up window, and we seem to be missing one of our salads."

After nodding his head apologetically but not saying anything to Brian, the man turned and yelled, "Carl!"

Moments later the drive-thru guy appeared. "This man didn't get one of his salads," the Hispanic employee explained.

Without saying a word, Carl disappeared for a moment, then came back. "Was that for Sharon?"

Patiently, Brian explained. "No, it was Leslie. We were here just fifteen minutes ago."

The clerk mumbled something barely audible that sounded like "Check be right back," and disappeared.

At that moment, the front door opened and Brian turned to see an older, vaguely familiar-looking man come in.

When the drive-thru guy returned, he was frowning. "I don't see an order for Leslie. Are you sure you . . ."

Before he could continue, Brian interrupted playfully, but with a mild hint of impatient sarcasm. "Yes, I'm sure. You don't think I came back down here just to scam you out of a salad, do you? This is the second time this has happened."

And then the man behind Brian interrupted the exchange. "Let me take care of this for you, sir."

Confused, Brian turned to see who was talking to him, and before he could say anything, the man continued. "I'm the owner of this place."

Then he turned to the employee. "Carl, go make me another large salad. And bring back a coupon for a free pizza."

Reaching out his hand for a shake, the older man explained to Brian, "Sorry about that. We're a little undermanned right now."

Brian estimated the guy's age to be around sixty-five, though it was hard to tell because his dark skin was so leathery and wrinkled, as though he'd spent a lot of time in the sun. And then Brian figured out why the man looked familiar. He was an older version of one of the two guys on the T-shirt.

"You must be Gene or Joe?" Brian asked politely.

The old man nodded. "I'm Joe."

For some reason, Brian had to ask the next question. "Where's Gene?"

"Somewhere in Florida, I think. He backed out of the partnership nineteen years ago, but I decided not to change the name. So, you've had this problem before, huh?"

Brian was a little hesitant now, not wanting to get anyone in trouble or to criticize this man's business. "Yeah, maybe once. But it might have been our fault."

"No," Joe said, shaking his head. "It's usually ours."

Brian felt bad for the old man. He decided to make small talk. "How long have you had this place, Joe?"

"Thirty-two years in February. It used to be fancier back in the seventies," he seemed a little embarrassed by the state of his restaurant. "But with the buildup of the casinos and all, we had to adjust. We don't do lunches anymore. Just dinner. And we cater to a little less formal clientele now. Skiers and hikers and bikers, you know."

Brian nodded.

At that moment Carl emerged from behind the counter.

"Here you go. Sorry about that." This time there was a slight, barely detectable hint of concern in his voice, which Brian attributed to the presence of the boss.

"Thank you," Brian responded, both to Carl and Joe. "I'm sure I'll see you again."

"I hope so." The old man smiled. "And we'll get your order right next time."

"No problem." Brian shook his hand again and left.

During the short drive home, Brian couldn't stop thinking about the restaurant and what it must be like to be Joe or Carl or the other indifferent-looking employees there.

What in the world gets those people out of bed in the morning?

FIRST SIP

Later that night Brian went out for a few groceries. Now that he was free of his crutches, any errand was a welcome one for him.

As he was leaving the store, his eye caught the front page of the *Wall Street Journal* on the newspaper stand. After scanning the headline section, he reluctantly decided to buy a copy to take home, well aware that he was playing with fire. He knew that Leslie would not be happy to know that he was indulging what she called his "business addiction."

Before Brian could make it to the register, he somehow found himself in the magazine aisle, adding copies of *BusinessWeek, Fortune,* and *Fast Company* to his stack of forbidden literature.

When he pulled up to his cabin, he carefully put the magazines and newspaper in the bottom of a grocery bag so that Leslie wouldn't see them. After she went to bed, Brian grabbed the stash and went to his favorite chair, eager to indulge his hunger for news about the world of business.

After less than half an hour with the *Journal,* Brian was ready to put it down and go to bed, disappointed that his deviant behavior hadn't yielded more of a thrill. Then he saw a small article on the third page of the Market section. The headline read, "Nike's FlexPro to Cut People, Products."

Brian devoured the story which detailed Nike's decision to lay off more than fifty people from the company it had acquired, and eliminate almost half the products that it manufactured. At the end of the article, it was mentioned that FlexPro's competitors were "rumored to be considering similar moves." Though the article didn't mention JMJ by name, Brian knew that his former company was certainly one of those competitors.

Knowing that he wasn't going to be able to sleep and that he had already violated the spirit of his agreement with his wife, Brian went to his computer. Casting aside his guilt, he went straight to his former company's new Web site where he learned that the sales and marketing departments were being moved away from Manteca to the parent company's headquarters outside Chicago.

Brian was furious.

He fired off an e-mail to Rick explaining that the decisions violated the spirit of the deal he had made with the medical company. He sent messages to the two members of his former executive team to tell them how upset he was that their jobs were being moved.

With adrenaline now running through his veins, Brian tore into his magazines with a vengeance, devouring anything and everything having to do with business. Though it had been just eight weeks since he retired, it felt like years.

Brian finally fell asleep in his chair at four in the morning, his magazines sprinkled next to him on the floor. When Leslie woke up a few hours later, she discovered him there, looking like an alcoholic surrounded by empty bottles.

Then the phone rang, and Brian began to stir. Before he knew what was happening, Leslie was handing him the cordless. "It's Rick Simpson." Leslie didn't need to say another word. The look on her face told Brian exactly how she felt.

OFF THE WAGON

Rick was calling in response to Brian's late night e-mail.

"Hey buddy. How's retirement treating you?"

Brian didn't elaborate. "Fine, thanks. I guess you got my note." It wasn't a question.

"Yeah. What are you doing up at two fifteen in the morning?"

"Rick, what the hell is going on over there? They're not supposed to be moving staff out of Manteca. That was part of the deal."

"Well, that's not necessarily true. They said they wouldn't shut down the plant there, and that they had no plans to move people. But that's standard for an acquisition. You know that."

"Yeah, but I told people they shouldn't be worried about their jobs."

Rick suspected that Brian's mood was as much a function of his general struggle with the transition to retirement as it was with the events at JMJ. So he decided to be gentle.

"Listen, Brian. Anyone who is adversely affected by this is going to get a nice severance package. That was part of the deal, which you did a great job negotiating. And compared to what Nike is doing with FlexPro, this is actually pretty mild."

Brian was momentarily speechless.

Rick kept talking. "I know how attached you were to that place, but you got a fair deal for JMJ, and now it's time to let go, my friend."

"Maybe." Brian took a breath and tried to convince himself that Rick was right. But he couldn't do it. "It's just that they're going to flush years of trust and loyalty down the toilet. They don't understand that that's what they paid for in the deal. I told you we should have found a buyer who understood us. We probably would have gotten more."

Rick should have said nothing, but as usual, he couldn't turn down a chance to debate, especially when his professional skills were being questioned. "No, they bought a factory, a brand name, a few patents, and a customer list. And they still have those things. And believe me. No one was going to pay you more than they did, because none of that touchy-feely stuff makes it to the bottom line."

Brian was now fully engaged, even angry. "You just don't get it, do you? The culture we built had more to do with our success than anything else. Those patents? Those products? The brand? Hell, those are a direct result of a bunch of people who loved their jobs."

"No," Rick countered, condescension creeping into his voice. "Those people loved their jobs because they were winning. And they were winning because you happened to have good products in the right market at the right time. All that other stuff is twenty-twenty hindsight bullshit."

For a moment Brian thought he was going to hang up on Rick. Luckily, the beep on the line gave him a reason to end the call more civilly. "That's my other line. I've got to go."

43

Before Rick could say "Me too," Brian clicked over to the incoming call.

It was Rob, his old head of marketing. He was calling to thank him for his e-mail, but to assure him that he had no hard feelings about the earlier-than-expected job change.

"We all figured this was going to happen sooner or later. Heck, plenty of people have already left, and like me, most of them already have jobs lined up. And with the exit package that you negotiated for us, I'm actually pretty happy with everything. Besides, things aren't the same around here anyway."

Brian was both relieved and heartbroken. "What about the folks in the factory?"

"Everything on the manufacturing side is staying here, so they'll be fine. I mean, it won't be as much fun for them, that's for sure. Some are probably going to leave just because they don't like the changes. But their jobs are relatively secure. There's even some talk about expansion."

After the call was over, Brian ate breakfast with Leslie and confessed the sordid details of his binge the night before. She convinced him to call Rick back and mend whatever needed to be patched up between them.

As usual, Rick was jovial and unaffected by it all—if not just a little indelicate.

After accepting Brian's apology, he made a suggestion. "You know, maybe you should become a counselor or something up there."

Brian was confused. "Why do you say that?"

"I don't know. You could put your interest in making people feel good about themselves to good use. I think you'd enjoy something like that. Less about the numbers. More about people."

Though he knew Rick was trying to be nice, Brian found himself getting frustrated again. He took a breath. "Rick, do you think that I enjoyed running JMJ?"

Rick tried to backtrack. "Yeah, sure, it's just that, I don't know, your passion for people would probably be more appreciated in another line of work. That's all."

Brian forced himself to be calm. He spoke slowly. "Okay, Rick. I'm going to explain this one more time. My interest in people is exactly why I liked being a CEO. That's why I was a good CEO."

For a long five seconds, there was an awkward silence on the line.

Rick finally spoke, unconvincingly. "Maybe you're right, Brian. Maybe I'm wrong. Who knows? We might look back two years from now and find that JMJ has crashed and burned because employees stop feeling so good about themselves and their jobs."

Brian was smiling when he asked his next question. "But you don't think so, do you?"

Rick chuckled, in a sheepish kind of way. "No I don't. But then again, I can be a real jerk sometimes."

Brian laughed, apologized again for his diatribe, and thanked his obnoxious friend for taking the time to indulge the frustration of a retired old CEO.

When he hung up, Brian felt a strange sense of determination to prove his former roommate wrong. He could not have guessed how that would play out, and what the next few months had in store for him.

IT POURS

The next day Brian promised his wife that he would renew his commitment to retirement, at least for a year. And then he went to the doctor.

His leg had not healed as well as they would have liked, and Brian was going to have to avoid any exercise for another six weeks. Certainly no skiing or hiking, and not even stationary cycling. No crutches, which was great, but no meaningful exercise other than walking.

Beside himself with frustration, Brian began to experience what felt like a bout of insanity.

And then it happened. One day as Leslie was out shopping, Brian grabbed the phone and made a call that would change his life, and that of his family, in a way that none of them could have imagined.

TAKE IN

Ayouthful voice that Brian didn't recognize answered the phone. "Gene and Joe's."

"Is Joe there?"

"No, I haven't seen him today. I guess he doesn't come in much on Mondays. But you might want to try tomorrow."

"Wait. Is there a number where I can reach him?"

"Oh, sure. Let's see. Here it is." He read the number to Brian. "Is there anything I can get for you, man? Something to eat maybe?"

Brian, surprised by the cheerful if not a little informal response, asked, "No, thanks. Are you new down there?"

"Yeah, this is my first day. How'd you know?"

"I just don't remember you, that's all. Anyway, thanks for the information."

Brian then dialed Joe's number and left a message.

Later that evening, while Leslie and Brian were watching *It's a Wonderful Life* for the twenty-fifth time during their twenty-eight years of marriage, the phone rang. Leslie, being a little more mobile than her sore husband, answered it.

"Yes, can I say who's calling? Sure."

With a puzzled look on her face, she explained. "It's someone name Joe Colombano, returning your call?"

Brian tried to react nonchalantly as though he wasn't the least bit interested in Joe Colombano or surprised that he was calling. "Right," he responded matter-of-factly.

"Who's Joe Colombano?" she asked.

Brian didn't want to lie to her, but he certainly wasn't ready to tell her the entire story. "Oh, it's a nice old guy I met down at that Italian restaurant. I think I might be able to help him with a problem he's having." He took the phone from Leslie and made his way toward one of the bedrooms.

She smiled at him as if to say, *well, that's nice of you,* and then asked, "You want me to pause this?"

"No, this should only take a minute, and I think I remember what happens."

She smiled again and returned to the movie.

THE MEETING

At nine o'clock the next morning, Brian put on a pair of khakis and a nice sweater and drove to Gene and Joe's. Only one car was in the parking lot—an old Toyota pickup truck with a camper shell on the back and a faded bumper sticker that said "Keep Tahoe Blue."

Walking through the front door, Brian saw Joe sitting at a table, going through receipts of some kind, and drinking coffee.

"Excuse me?"

The old man turned, surprised by his guest. "Well hello there. You're the guy with the missing salad, aren't you?"

Brian nodded.

"What can I do for you? I'm afraid we won't be open for another—"

Brian politely interrupted the wrinkled entrepreneur. "I'm Brian Bailey. I spoke to you on the phone last night."

Joe looked puzzled. "That was you?"

"That's right."

"Oh. I guess I was expecting something, or someone, different."

Clearing his papers from the center of the table, the old man regrouped. "Sit down, Brian."

Brian took his résumé from a folder and handed it to Joe, who, after reading for a few seconds with a puzzled look on his face, started laughing.

"What is this, some kind of prank? What can I do for you, Mr. Bailey?"

"It's no joke, Joe. I'm here to apply for your weekend manager position."

Joe looked down at the résumé again. "Is all this true?"

Brian nodded, clearly serious.

"Okay then. I guess I have to ask the question. Why in the world would you be applying for a job here?"

Before Brian could answer, Joe continued, as though he had figured something out.

"Did you just get out of prison or something? Or rehab?"

Brian smiled and shook his head. "No sir. Just recuperating from a skiing accident and trying to enjoy retirement."

"And how does being the weekend manager at Gene and Joe's fit into the plans of a retired C E O?" Joe pronounced the letters as though he were unimpressed by them, or that he hadn't used them many times before. Brian decided it was the latter.

"Well, it doesn't, I guess. It's just something I want to do."

Joe paused to consider the situation, still staring at the résumé, and then began to shake his head. "No. I'm sorry. This has to be some kind of prank." He handed the résumé back across the table.

Brian didn't take it, so Joe continued, almost indignant, but in a friendly kind of way. "You expect me to believe that a big-time executive like you is going to come to work here for nine dollars an hour? I'm no idiot, mister."

"Not only do I expect you to, I can't imagine you turning me down. I have to be the best candidate you've got right now."

"That's not true." Joe responded emphatically. "You're the only candidate I have right now. And I'm still not going to hire you."

"Why not?"

"For one, because I don't believe you. And two, even if you were serious, you'd quit within twenty-four hours, forty-eight, tops."

Now Brian was beginning to enjoy the bizarre interview. "What do I have to do to convince you that I'm serious?"

Joe thought about it. "I don't know." He looked around the quiet restaurant as though an answer might suddenly appear. "You tell me."

Brian smiled in a sly kind of way. "Okay, how about if I work for a week with no wages. If I'm still here after that, then you can pay me what you owe me from the first week. If not, you can keep it all."

After a few seconds of consideration, Joe shook his head. "Come on now," he looked at the résumé again, "Brian, what's wrong with you? This just doesn't make any sense."

Now Brian became a little more serious. "You're right, Joe. It doesn't. But I have my reasons. And I need something to do. If not here, then I'll go to the next place that's looking to hire someone. I'm betting someone is going to be pretty glad to have me."

Brian, sensing that Joe could see his point, continued.

"And if I don't do a good job, then fire me. But if I do a good job, then I'll expect to be rewarded."

For the next twenty minutes, the two men went back and forth, with Brian at one time teasing that he would sue Gene and Joe's for discrimination against a guy with a bum knee. Joe accused Brian of having every ulterior motive possible, from being an undercover agent for the Food and Drug Administration to a host of the TV show Candid Camera.

Though it wasn't easy, Brian eventually wore the old man down, but at a price he hadn't expected.

With everything finally ironed out, Joe took a deep breath and, with what appeared to be complete earnestness, said "Well, I don't usually like to take a chance on a guy who didn't finish college."

Brian laughed as his new boss reached out his hand. "But I guess I'll make an exception. Welcome to Gene and Joe's. You can start Thursday night."

Brian shook his hand as though Joe had just given him his first job, and left with the strangest sense of victory he had ever experienced. But any feelings of excitement disappeared when he thought about what he would say to his wife.

SANITY CHECK

Leslie was on the phone when Brian came home. As soon as she saw her husband, she wrapped up the call. "Yeah, he just walked in. I'll tell him you said hi. I've got to go too. Bye, honey, I love you."

Leslie hung up and greeted her husband excitedly. "That was Lynne, and she's got some big news."

"Didn't she want to talk to me?"

"She had to go to class. She said she'll call you tonight. Anyway, she had another interview today with Hilton, which went well, and she thinks she's going to get an offer."

"That's great." Though Brian would normally have been elated by the news, his pending conversation was muting some of his excitement.

"And guess which properties she might be able to choose from?" Leslie didn't give him a chance to guess. "Portland, San Antonio," she paused, "and South Lake Tahoe!"

"You're kidding?"

"Nope. Wouldn't that be incredible?"

Brian badly wanted to postpone the conversation he was planning to have, but figured that he might as well take advantage of Leslie's mood.

"That would be fantastic."

Leslie knew her husband well enough to know that he wasn't as excited as she would have expected. "What's wrong?"

"Nothing. It's just that I have some news too."

Leslie seemed eager to hear.

"I was just at Gene and Joe's, the Italian place."

Leslie nodded.

Brian looked at the ground, "I'm going to start helping them out down there."

Leslie was neither excited nor disappointed. "That's great. What exactly are you going to be doing? Marketing or something?"

"No. Not exactly. I'm actually going to be doing some management stuff for Joe."

"What does that mean?" Leslie hadn't quite figured it out. "Consulting?"

"No. I'm going to be running the restaurant for him three nights a week."

Brian would never forget the look on his wife's face. In a matter of nanoseconds, it seemed to transform from interest to confusion to mild shock.

At first Leslie was too stunned to say anything. Finally, she began with the obvious question. "Are you serious?" She could see that he was, but had to ask anyway.

Brian nodded, like a twelve-year-old admitting that he ditched school.

With a mixture of dismay and pity in her voice, Leslie continued. "Why? Why in the world? What are you doing, honey?"

"It's complicated, Leslie."

"So you think I'm not capable of understanding?"

"No, it's that I'm not sure I'm capable of explaining it."

"Is it that you're bored with me? You have to know that this makes me feel pretty bad."

The look on Brian's face was one of incredulity. "No, no. It's not that at all. I'm loving spending time with you. It's just that, I don't know, I need to be *doing* something. Managing something. Do you know how long it's been since I had no real problems to solve in my life? I just can't turn that off."

"So you're going to be an employee at a fast-food joint?"

"No, not technically."

Leslie was confused.

"I'm actually part owner of the place."

Her mouth dropped.

DEFENSE

What? Why would you—" She didn't finish the sentence.

Brian laughed, but in a guilty, almost scared kind of way. "Because that's the only way I could convince him to hire me. But I'm just a minority partner, and it only cost me twelve thousand dollars. And I figure that if I do a good job, maybe I can turn that into thirteen or fourteen."

Leslie refused to acknowledge the joke. "I still don't get it. Why not do charity work? Or volunteer at church? Or heck, move to Africa and be a missionary? Why this?"

"I know it sounds weird—"

She interrupted him. "No, it doesn't sound weird. It *is* weird."

Brian looked at the ground for a moment while Leslie waited for a response. When he looked up again, she could see he was a little hurt. She listened.

"I know it doesn't make sense right now, Les. And yes, I did think of doing volunteer work down at church, or starting a nonprofit."

Again, Leslie jumped in, almost pleading. "See, that would be great. Why not do that?"

Brian now became a little more intense. "Because that's not what I do. I'm not an envelope stuffer or a doughnut hander-outer. I'm a manager, Les. I think it's my gift. I know that sounds corny, but I think it's true. Some people are naturals at painting or playing the piano or writing poetry or playing baseball. I'm good at managing."

Leslie considered her husband's words, and let him continue. "And I actually believe that the best way I can help people is by managing them. I don't build houses or grow corn or design aqueducts. I help people in their jobs."

Leslie knew that her husband was sincere, and that what he was saying made some sense, but she was still confused. "But why that silly Italian restaurant? Why not a regular business?"

"Because it's right down the street, and it's only three nights a week. We're not moving back to the Bay Area or anything. You won't even know I'm gone."

Brian could tell that Leslie was starting to buy in, so he let it all out.

"Leslie, I really want to see if I can figure out how to make this quirky little Italian fast-food drive-thru thrive. I saw the people who work there walking around like they're in a coma, and I remember when I first joined JMJ and saw some of the same things there. If I can give these people something to look forward to in their jobs, then that would be pretty neat."

Leslie paused, considering the situation. "Does this have something to do with that butthead Rick?"

Brian laughed, not accustomed to his wife being quite so childishly crude. "Well, I'd be lying if I said no. But it's more than that. It's about proving to myself that JMJ wasn't a fluke, and that all the time and energy I put into people there had something to do with the success we had."

Leslie was about to throw in the towel, and then decided to make one more attempt at sanity. "But it's a pizzeria."

"Exactly. Don't the people who work there deserve to have a tolerable job as much as anyone else?"

Leslie took a few long seconds to consider her husband's point. Then she shook her head and unsuccessfully fought off a smile. "You're a strange, strange man, Brian Bailey."

All Brian could do was agree.

PART THREE

❖

The
Experiment

COLD FEET

The reality of his decision began to strike Brian when he woke up on Thursday morning. But it wasn't until he put on his "Gene and Joe's" T-shirt that it completely hit home.

As he was heading out the door, he looked at Leslie and said, "What am I doing?"

Leslie smiled, and demonstrated yet again why Brian had been so lucky to marry her almost thirty years ago. "Because, as you said, it's why God put you on earth. You're a manager. And a leader. You can't help it."

"But look at me." He turned toward a mirror in the entryway of the cabin. "I'm wearing a shirt that says 'Pizza and Pasta. Here, There, Everywhere.'"

They both laughed, in an almost pathetic way.

Leslie pulled him through. "Listen. This is no different from college. You're about to begin the world's best graduate course on management. It's all about learning."

Her pep talk looked to be working, so she continued. "And I'm telling you the absolute truth here. I actually think it's pretty cool. I wish I could come with you."

That was exactly what Brian needed to hear.

PAST-DUE DILIGENCE

As he pulled up to the restaurant he had driven by dozens of times, he decided that somehow this time it looked different. He noticed the peeling paint and a broken window on the side of the building that he didn't recall seeing before. Gene and Joe's, as it turned out, was a little dirtier and more tired than he had remembered.

Saying a silent prayer as he unbuckled his seatbelt, Brian climbed out of the car and headed across the almost empty parking lot toward the front door of the restaurant.

Inside, Joe was at the cash register while a twenty-something Hispanic man was slicing vegetables on the counter behind him.

"Afternoon, Brian. You're early." Joe's greeting didn't sound at all special, as though Brian had been coming to work there for years.

"Hey Joe, can I talk to you for a second?"

Joe closed the register. "Sure." The two of them sat down at a nearby table.

"So, is this the part where you tell me that you're not going through with this?" Joe asked, a little sarcastically.

Though Brian had actually considered bailing out a few times in the past thirty seconds, he wasn't going to back out now. "You think I'd be wearing this T-shirt if I came down here to quit?"

Joe laughed.

"Besides, I can't quit a restaurant that I own, now, can I?"

"That's right, I guess. So what do you need?"

"I want you to tell me what's going on with the business."

"Shouldn't you ask a question like that before you buy a company?" Joe asked sarcastically.

Brian smiled. "Yeah, I guess so. I suppose I'm not very smart. Anyway, what's the situation?"

Joe thought about it. "Well, about eighty percent of our business is done on the weekends, when you'll be here. On a yearly financial basis, we usually come in just a little under or over breakeven. December, February, July, and August, the peak vacation months, are when we can make a pretty healthy profit. If we get a lot of snow, we tend to make money for the year. If not, we don't."

"Okay, aside from the seasonal nature of the business, what's your biggest challenge?"

Joe shrugged. "I don't know. I suppose part of it is me. I'm not all that interested in making a lot more money, as long as I get time to ski and fish and golf. I'm not trying to be Donald Trump here."

Brian nodded. "Okay, but assume that you did want to make more money. Do you think you could?"

Joe didn't hesitate. "A little, maybe. Probably not much. I mean, we're a bit off the beaten path over here, and my employees are a motley crew. At least the ones who stick around."

"So turnover's a problem?"

Joe nodded in exasperation.

"Why do you think?" Brian asked.

"Heck if I know. Most of these people aren't exactly go-getters, if you know what I mean."

"What are they, then?"

"I don't know. So many of them come and go, it's hard to keep straight. I don't really know what they do in their spare time, and that's probably a good thing because I'm guessing some of it isn't legal." He laughed.

Trying to be polite, Brian persisted. "But you must have some idea why people leave."

Joe thought about it for a second. "Come on, Brian. None of them are getting rich or solving the world's problems here. It's manual labor, really. Which is why getting them to give a damn, not to mention show up on time," he looked at his watch, "is a battle in itself."

"If they did give a damn or come to work on time, what is it you'd want them to do?"

Joe shrugged. "How about make sure that when a lady orders a salad, she gets it?" He laughed. "That would be a good start."

The phone rang. "But maybe you can figure something out. That's why I'm paying you the big bucks." He got up from the table, slapped Brian on the back, and went to pick up the phone.

STAFF

s the Thursday night dinner crew started to arrive, Brian introduced himself. Most of them had no knowledge that a new manager was coming on board, nor did they seem to care. Offering no explanation for their tardiness, they went about their jobs without fanfare.

Brian spent the rest of the time before the restaurant opened learning the names and job responsibilities of the nine employees who made up the weekend crew.

Joaquin served as the primary cook, handling all meat entrees—chicken, fish, and beef—and pastas. He was a short, stocky Guatemalan with a large moustache and a scar on the side of his face. He spoke extremely broken English, and with a thick accent.

Kenny was a prep cook of sorts, handling everything from salads to pizzas to gelato. At 6'7" and less than two hundred pounds, he was the thinnest human being that Brian had ever seen. His accent, part Oklahoma and part hillbilly, made Kenny almost as difficult to understand as Joaquin.

Tristan, the "new" employee who'd answered the phone when Brian called about the job, worked the counter, answered the phone, helped customers find tables, and did everything related to bills and making change. He looked about seventeen but was actually a youthful twenty-five.

Salvador, a tiny, quiet man from Mexico, washed dishes and cleaned the kitchen and bathroom whenever it was needed.

Carl handled the drive-thru and helped Joaquin and Salvador in the kitchen. As Brian had already noticed, Carl seemed to be in his forties. He wore a wedding ring and had a tattoo of a peace sign on his forearm.

Harrison was a big guy with a red beard, and he made most of the home deliveries, driving an old Chevy Impala with a magnetic "Gene and Joe's" placard on the door. Brian remembered seeing him at his home delivering food once or twice.

Joleen was an attractive blonde waitress, an early twenty-something with a diamond-looking stud in her nose. She handled half of the dining room.

Patty handled the other half. She seemed to be almost thirty, though Brian decided she worked hard to look younger.

Next, there was *Migo,* the young guy who was prepping food when Brian came in search of his lost salad. His real name was Miguel, but everyone knew him by his nickname. Migo seemed to be something of a utility man, filling in wherever he was needed, which included making pizzas, busing tables, and running the drive-thru.

And of course there was Joe, who dove in when things were busy or when someone was sick or decided to quit without giving notice, or when something went wrong. And plenty usually went wrong.

OPENING NIGHT

Brian's anxiety about the ridiculousness of his situation didn't fade until the restaurant opened and customers started to come in. It was only then that he began to feel like he was part of a business again. Sure, it was a fraction of the size of the organization he had run at JMJ, but it had employees and customers and for now that was enough.

The night was a typical Thursday for Gene and Joe's, busier than anyone who had been in the empty place during the day could have imagined. And while the clientele didn't arrive wearing ties and sport coats, they were not particularly unsophisticated, just informal and weary after a long day of skiing or whatever it was they had been doing.

Joe told his new manager to spend his first night observing as much as he could about the operation, and learning how to work the register. Brian did that quickly, and found plenty of opportunities to pitch in by busing tables and shuttling pizza and pasta from the kitchen to the dining room.

The night went by faster than he could have guessed. Because the restaurant was located off the beaten path and away from the hotels, closing time was relatively early. So at 10:15, more than an hour after the last customer had gone, Brian and Migo shut the place down. Joe had offered to let Brian go earlier, but he insisted on staying until closing.

As Brian locked the front door of the restaurant and turned toward his car, he was surprised to see that there was another vehicle in the parking lot, right next to his. As he came closer, he realized that it was Leslie's car, but she was nowhere to be seen. Then he noticed that she was sitting inside Brian's Explorer, reading a book.

When he opened the door, he was greeted by his smiling wife and a burst of hot air from the car's heater. "What are you doing here?" he asked.

"Just waiting for my boyfriend after his first day of work. Let's go get dessert."

DEBRIEF

Brian and Leslie drove into South Lake Tahoe and found a train-themed diner called Mountain Express. It was clean and fairly crowded.

As they sat down at a table, Leslie dove right in. "So?" She was certainly more curious about her husband's new job than Brian would have guessed when he first told her about it.

"Well, it wasn't what I expected, that's for sure."

"In a good or bad way?"

Brian had to think about it. "Both, I guess."

She frowned. "Really? You're not going to quit, are you?"

"No, it's not that bad. The work itself wasn't horrible. In fact, there's something gratifying about doing real manual work for a change."

"What was the bad part, then?"

"It was just more depressing than I would have thought."

"How so?"

He shrugged. "I don't know. I mean, I did my time at Captain Hamburger's and Carrows, so I wasn't expecting it to be an amusement park. But this was more like a morgue. I can't believe they do this every night."

"Maybe that's just the nature of working in a restaurant these days."

Brian frowned. "I don't think so." He felt like he was trying to talk himself into his answer. "I certainly hope not."

"Do they work hard?"

He hesitated. "Yeah, but with no sense of engagement. It's like they don't care what they're doing, and frankly, the customers don't seem to care much either. It's just a place to get warm food."

He looked around the restaurant trying to find someone to wait on them. "It looks like this place might have the same problem. Where's our waitress?"

As they gave up searching and returned to scanning the dessert menus that were already on the table, they were interrupted.

"I'm really sorry to keep you guys waiting so long."

It was a waiter, maybe twenty years old, sporting the saddest mustache Leslie had ever seen. Smiling enough to show a shiny set of braces on his teeth, he introduced himself. "I'm Jack. What can I get for you?"

"What do you recommend, Jack?" Leslie was always open to suggestions.

"If you're looking for dessert, I like the peach cobbler and the German chocolate cake."

"What about the apple pie?" Brian wanted to know.

"Nah. That's not one of our better ones. I think my wife makes it better."

Leslie looked at Brian as if to say, *he has a wife?* "How about the Tiramisu?"

Now Jack-the-waiter wrinkled his nose. "You know, I just don't like Tiramisu. So I'm the wrong guy to ask. But I have to admit that I've never heard anyone rave about it."

Before the Baileys could make their decision, the waiter asked. "You guys on vacation?"

Leslie was more of an extrovert than her husband, and she usually answered first. "No, we live up here."

"Skiers?"

"Used to be. He blew out his knee." Leslie motioned toward her husband.

"Bummer." Jack seemed to mean it. "Is it serious?"

Now Brian joined in. "Enough to put me out of action for the year."

The friendly waiter winced in empathy. "You must be missing it a lot."

Brian nodded.

"Have you tried snowmobiling?"

Having decided on her order, Leslie now put her menu down and rejoined the conversation. "I've always wanted to do that."

Brian looked at her with amusement. "Really?"

"Sure, it looks fun."

Jack egged her on. "You can rent snowmobiles a few blocks from here, and after fifteen minutes of instruction, you're good to go, even with a bum knee. And you can ride together, for less than two hundred bucks a day. I know that's a lot of money, but if you can afford it—" He didn't finish the sentence.

Leslie was genuinely grateful for the advice. "Well, thank you, Jack."

Brian smiled, both at the spunky waiter and his equally spunky wife. He thought the prospect of going snowmobiling with her sounded pretty good too.

They placed their order and let Jack go.

"Maybe I was wrong about working in a restaurant." Leslie announced gleefully. "You should hire that guy."

"That's exactly what I was thinking. I ought to offer him a job tonight." Brian was serious.

Leslie was a little surprised. "I was joking, Brian. You can't just go hire him. You've only been there one day. You can't just show up on your second day and say, 'hey everyone, meet Jack.'"

Brian smiled. "Yes I can. I'm an owner. Remember?"

She laughed. "Don't you think you should talk it over with Joe first?"

"Are you kidding? Joe wouldn't know a good employee if one bit him on the butt. That's probably why things are so bad down there?"

At that moment, another guy, a few years older than Jack, came to the table carrying the coffee and hot chocolate that Brian and Leslie had ordered. "Jack will be here in a few minutes with your pie."

Leslie decided to be curious. "Excuse me. Do you know Jack, our waiter?"

The guy hesitated. "Sure. Why? Is something wrong?"

"No, not at all. In fact, he's very nice. I was just wondering how long he's been working here."

"A little over a year. He moved up here from Reno to go to a community college, and got married a few months ago. He's one of the better ones I have."

"Are you the owner of this place?"

"No, just a manager."

Now Brian jumped in, a little surprised. "You said he's *one* of the better ones you have. Are there others like him?"

The manager thought about it. "Yeah, a few of the others are good like Jack. Most aren't quite as comfortable with customers, though."

Brian laughed. "Can I ask where you find them?"

The manager shrugged. "I think the owner puts an ad in the newspaper. That's how I found my job."

"Does he pay more than the other restaurants around here?"

The guy looked as though he had never thought about it before. "I don't really know. But I don't think so. I think we make better tips than some of the other places, but that's about it."

Just then Jack came back with the food, and the manager smiled and left the table with an encouraging "enjoy your dessert."

As Jack put the plates down, Brian decided to be bold.

"Jack, how do you like working here?"

The young waiter didn't hesitate. "I like it a lot." Then he corrected himself, almost embarrassed. "I mean, it's probably not what I'll do forever. But it's actually a really good job." He smiled like he meant it.

"Why do you think you like it so much?"

Jack glanced over at two tables that had just been seated in his station, but tried to focus on the conversation with his current customers. "I don't know. You should probably ask Jeremy."

"Who's Jeremy?"

"My manager. The guy who brought you the hot chocolate." Jack glanced over at his tables again. "Excuse me, folks, I need to go take their order. I'd be glad to come back over in a few minutes if—"

Brian waved his hand. "No, don't worry about it. Thanks for your time and your help, Jack."

As the young waiter walked away, Leslie asked, half jokingly, half seriously, "Why didn't you offer him a job?"

Brian nodded. "Because there is no way he'd take it."

Leslie was a little confused, so Brian explained himself.

"Why in the world would a hardworking, cheerful young guy like that want to work at a depressing place like Gene and Joe's? And I'd feel horrible even trying to take Jack out of here. I need to make some changes there before I can think about hiring anyone new."

"What kind of changes?" Leslie wanted to know.

Brian smiled excitedly. "I'm not exactly sure yet, but I can't wait to find out."

At that moment, Leslie could see how much her husband had needed a project like this one.

LIP BITING

Though he wanted to dive in and start making changes right away, Brian decided that he would force himself to observe one more night at the restaurant before coming to any conclusions. It turned out to be a long night.

First, he watched as three different drive-thru customers returned because of incomplete orders. One of them had to come back twice on the same order! And it wasn't so much that the orders were wrong that bothered Brian, it was that it didn't seem to bother anyone, least of all Carl.

Treatment of customers by Joleen and Patty ranged from friendliness to indifference to surliness, depending on the mood of the customers and the waitresses themselves. Only Migo seemed to take pride in his work, doing whatever his coworkers asked of him without hesitation or complaint.

As the evening went on, Brian became more and more amazed that Gene and Joe's had stayed in business at all. One particular incident captured the mess of the restaurant best.

It was three minutes before nine o'clock, the closing time for the restaurant on a Friday night. As he was counting the register, Brian suddenly heard someone in the front of the restaurant yell, "Autobus!" Ironically, it was Carl, not one of the Hispanic employees, who sounded the alarm in Spanish.

At that moment the restaurant came alive, as though a bomb had gone off. Within ten seconds, the front door was locked, the lights in the dining room were out, and most of the chairs were turned over onto the tables. The employees who remained seemed to be hiding in the corners of the building, away from the windows.

At first Brian thought that the place was about to be robbed. He went to the drive-thru window and looked outside. There in the parking lot was a bus. On the windows of the bus were signs, written with soap. "Go Rams! Beat the Tigers! Go LHS!"

Brian watched as the front door of the bus opened, and two men exited. They headed for the front door of Gene and Joe's, but as they got closer, they stopped. Checking their watches, the men shook their heads and made their way back to the bus. A few other adults had already gotten off, but the two scouts informed them that the place was closed, and they got back on. Finally, the bus pulled away, heading toward the lights of South Lake Tahoe.

As soon as the bus was gone, the employees in the restaurant seemed to breathe a collective sigh of relief and let out a muffled cheer. It was the most passion that Brian had seen from them in two days.

"What was that all about?" Brian asked, looking in the direction of Patty and Kenny. The relief in the room seemed to be tempered a bit by the question.

Finally, Kenny explained. "Two months ago that bus came in here ten minutes before closing time and stayed until ten thirty."

Patty finished for him. "They're a bunch of basketball moms and dads from the high school down the road in Lakeview. Whenever we see them coming, we try to close up fast."

Brian couldn't believe that they weren't the slightest bit embarrassed by what they were telling him.

Wishing he'd had the presence of mind to go out and invite the busload of people into the restaurant, the former CEO decided that he had seen enough and was ready to start making changes. Saturday night would mark the beginning of a new experience for the employees of Gene and Joe's.

ENGAGEMENT

Brian arrived at work early the next day, and asked Joe to do the same. More than an hour before any other employees arrived, the two co-owners sat down in the dining room to talk.

Joe started. "I hope you're not asking for your money back. Because I made it real clear that if you quit, you couldn't pull your investment out."

Brian laughed. "I'm not quitting, and I'm not asking for my money back."

Joe was relieved, which made it easier for Brian to continue.

"But I am asking you to let me make some changes around here."

Joe laughed. "Well, you've only been here two days. But be my guest." Then he paused. "What kind of changes are you thinking about? Like the menu or the décor?"

Brian had to fight hard to avoid laughing, both at Joe's choice of the word *décor* to describe the tacky interior of the old restaurant and at his pronunciation of the word (which sounded like deckore).

"No, I'm thinking more about managing people."

Joe frowned slightly. "What do you mean? You want to fire somebody?"

"No, nothing like that." Then Brian thought about it. "Although if that were the right thing to do, I might want to do that too. But that's not what I'm thinking."

Brian didn't want Joe to feel criticized, so he chose his words carefully. "I want to give employees a little clearer sense of what is expected of them."

That didn't seem to register with Joe, nor did it seem to concern him, which Brian decided was okay. He continued. "So, I was hoping that you could help me get the restaurant ready now, so that when the staff gets here, I can have a meeting with them."

Again, Joe's response was somewhere between indifferent and amenable. "Okay. Let's get to it."

The unlikely business partners prepared Gene and Joe's for the Saturday evening crowd. They swept floors, cleaned counters, chopped pizza ingredients, and stocked supplies. They even did a handful of other things—like straighten out the walk-in refrigerator and wash the menus thoroughly—that Brian decided hadn't been done for more than a few months.

By the time workers started arriving, the place was a little shinier than normal, something that was noticeable to even the most disinterested employee.

That would be Carl. "Who did all this stuff?" he asked.

Joe responded. "Me and Brian. And it only took us about forty-five minutes."

"So what are we supposed to do now?" he asked.

"I think you're having a meeting. I'm going to the movies."

And with that, Joe left, leaving Carl looking more confused than normal.

STAFF MEETING

Brian asked everyone to get something to drink and come into the dining room. Though there was no real policy, Joe tended to frown on employees getting fountain drinks for themselves until after closing time. Brian didn't know that, nor would he have cared.

When everyone was seated except for Migo, who had yet to arrive, the new manager began. He admitted to Leslie later that he was a little nervous, not knowing how these people would respond. He hadn't feared a revolt or anything like that. It was the prospect of complete indifference that somehow frightened him the most.

Deciding not to be clever or subtle, Brian got right to the point. "How many of you like your jobs?"

Nothing. People just looked at one another as though Brian had asked the question in Russian.

"Come on now, everybody. Show of hands. How many like your jobs?"

Slowly, every hand in the room went up, but with no conviction.

Brian smiled. "Okay, let me be clearer. I'm not asking how many of you want to keep your jobs. I'm not going to fire someone because they don't raise their hand."

Realizing that the people staring at him had no reason to trust him, Brian rephrased the question. "How about this? How many people here get excited about coming to work? How many of you are in a really good mood when you're driving here?"

Brian might as well have asked them if they liked being beaten with a stick. No one raised their hand, and more than a few of them actually laughed out loud.

Patty didn't raise her hand, but she blurted out a comment. "Well, I've got three little kids at home, so I'm just excited to get out of the house." Everyone laughed. "But I'd rather not be coming *here*."

Brian laughed along with everyone else in the room.

Carl joined in, unprompted. "I actually get kind of depressed when I wake up on Thursday mornings, because I know that I'm going to be here a lot for the rest of the week."

His colleagues seemed surprised by his frank admission.

Brian refocused the conversation. "Well, I'm here to tell you that my job is to get you to like your jobs. To look forward to coming to work."

The looks on the faces around the room were a mix of distrust, confusion, and boredom.

Brian knew better than to expect that this "motley crew" would embrace his ideas right away and throw their new leader on his shoulders and parade him around the dining room like Norma Rae.

"I realize that you think I'm nuts. But here's the thing. I honestly believe that if you like your jobs more, the business will do better."

"Is there something in it for us?" asked Harrison, politely.

Brian wanted to scream at his delivery guy. *How about not being miserable? How about making your life a little better and having pride in your work? Don't you think that would be a good thing for you and your family and friends? Or do you enjoy having the life sucked out of you every time you put on that damn Gene and Joe's T-shirt?!*

But he knew that these people had no reason to trust or believe him, not without a tangible incentive. "Well, for the next two months, everyone here on the weekend shift is going to get one dollar more per hour."

Eyes lit up, giving Brian the perfect opportunity to turn the screws on them.

"But that's only if everyone goes along with the plan. If just one person blows it off, then the hourly dollar goes away. Okay?"

For the first time since he had been there, Brian felt a sense of commitment, albeit barely detectable, from the staff. "But remember, I'm going to have you do some things that you've never done before. Got it?"

Tristan's hand went up, calming the mood for a moment. "You're not going to ask us to do anything illegal, are you?"

Brian laughed, and then realized that Tristan was serious. "No, no. Nothing illegal. Just different."

Others in the room laughed in amusement and relief, and Brian continued.

"The first is that we need to start coming to work on time."

As if on cue, the door opened and Migo came in. Everyone laughed nervously at the coincidence. The bizarre scene—the meeting, the laughter, the particularly clean restaurant—stunned Migo.

Brian knew that assurance would probably go a lot further than reprimand. "Have a seat, Migo. We were just talking about the importance of getting to work on time."

Everyone laughed again, but before Migo could get an excuse out of his mouth, Brian finished. "But I'm not talking about you in particular, and you don't need to tell me why you're late. No one's in trouble. This is about the future."

Migo accepted the absolution and sat down.

"But from now on, I need everyone here when they're supposed to be here. If there is a problem, call ahead and let me know." He paused. "And problems really ought to be rare."

Just as it looked like no one was going to react, Joaquin raised his hand. Brian pointed to him, and the Guatemalan cook said something in Spanish, in the direction of Migo, who translated.

"He wants to know if he can come in a little early on some nights, and a little later on others. He works the day shift at a gas station and it's sometimes hard to make the schedules fit."

The other employees seemed a little surprised by the boldness of the question, and were watching intently to see how the new manager would respond. Brian felt a quiet sense of shame that it hadn't even occurred to him that his employees might have other jobs.

He thought about it for a second. *"Porque no? Si puedes preparar en tiempo, yo digo, si?"* The Hispanic employees in the room seemed as surprised by Brian's ability to speak Spanish as they were by his answer.

Again, Migo translated, but this time for those who only spoke English. "He says, 'Why not? If you can prepare your work on time, I say it's fine.'" He looked at Brian to get his approval for the translation, and Brian nodded.

Now everyone in the room seemed almost stunned by their new manager's answer.

Brian decided that Joe had probably not been terribly open to their suggestions. He went on. "Okay, in addition to being on time, I want everyone here to start measuring what you're doing. I believe in the old saying that if you can't measure something, you can't improve it."

Knowing that this wouldn't make complete sense to everyone on his staff, Brian continued. "And don't worry. I'll be helping you figure out what you should be measuring, and how we're going to go about doing it. In fact, for most of you, that will start tonight."

Brian felt like he had said enough, and that actions would ultimately speak louder than words. "Okay, we've got a few minutes before opening. Let's get ready."

After everyone scattered, Brian took a moment to explain what was going on to Migo, who seemed genuinely eager about the whole thing, even before he found out about the increase in pay. Then the new manager began to put his program into effect. He decided to start with his biggest challenge: Carl.

FIRST TEST

Saturday night at Gene and Joe's was fairly crowded, mostly with weary skiers and assorted locals looking for a quick, informal dinner. The drive-thru window, something that never made much sense to Brian, was surprisingly busy on Saturday nights, especially with skiers heading back toward Reno.

The poster child for apathy at the restaurant, Carl essentially had three responsibilities; he took orders from customers, assembled the orders with the help of the kitchen staff, and handed over the food and collected payment for it. None of which he did very well.

Carl was not particularly responsive, accurate, or pleasant in his role at the drive-thru, but Joe had never felt like that part of the restaurant was important. "How much difference does it really make?" he'd told Brian.

However, Brian had noticed that when Carl made a mistake—something that was not terribly rare—it often set off a chain reaction throughout the restaurant. Joaquin might have to prepare a special order. Tristan might have to sort out the problem if the unhappy customer came to the front desk. And Joe would often find himself apologizing and asking other staff members to do something to make up for the problem. As a result, everything else would fall behind a little, creating back-logs and crises.

Though he had already given some thought to how he would make Carl's job more measurable, Brian wanted to give the guy a chance to come up with something on his own. At a point when no cars were in the drive-thru, Brian pulled Carl aside and asked Migo to keep an eye on the window.

When they were sitting down in the dining room, Brian began. "Carl, what would be a good way to measure whether you're doing a good job?"

Carl looked at him blankly and shrugged. "I don't know."

Brian tried again. "Let's say it's the end of the night and everything is closed out, how would you know that you had a good night at the window?"

Carl thought about it a little more. "The number of cars or orders that came through, maybe? Or the amount of time they had to wait?"

Brian nodded, patiently. "Okay, those would be all right. Of course, you don't really control the volume of customers that come through. That would be a good measure of how *busy* you were, maybe, but not of how well you were doing your job."

Carl seemed to understand the logic and nodded his agreement.

Brian continued. "The time that people wait might be a good one. But again, it depends on a lot of things outside your control. Like how well the guys in the kitchen are cranking out orders."

Again Carl agreed. "What do you think?"

Brian was glad to provide some direction. "I'm thinking that the number of orders you do without errors would be a good start."

Without the slightest bit of defensiveness (or enthusiasm), Carl nodded. "That's a good one."

"And I'm also thinking that you need something to measure that says you're dealing with customers in a positive way, so they'll want to come back again."

"Okay." The way Carl said it seemed to indicate that he didn't really understand what that might mean.

Brian went on. "What about if you make a note of the number of times you make people smile when they come through the drive-thru?"

It was as though Brian had asked Carl to climb through the window and give his customers back rubs. "Smile?"

"Sure. Why not?" Brian asked. "That's a pretty good indication that they're happy, and it's definitely within your control."

Carl was considering it.

"And if you could get one of them to actually laugh, that would be worth four smiles."

"I don't know. That seems pretty weird."

"Come on. You don't have to tell jokes or anything. Unless you want to. Just try smiling at them and asking a question or two. I'm betting that will work. Heck, ask them how skiing was, or where they're headed."

Either Carl seemed to realize that it was doable, or he remembered that the dollar per hour increase in his pay was riding on this. In any case, he nodded his head in a way that said, "Okay, I'll do it."

"So why don't you get one of those big placemats over there and make a score sheet on the back. Keep it next to the window, and write down how many errors you make in orders, and how many smiles you get from people."

"Don't you want someone else to do the counting?"

Brian was confused. "Why?"

"How do you know I won't cheat?"

Brian wanted to laugh, but maintained a serious demeanor. "Because I don't think you're that kind of person." He then looked around as though he wanted to make sure no one was listening, and explained in a hushed tone. "Besides, I've installed secret cameras all over the restaurant, and I'll be able to see everything."

And at that moment Brian saw Carl smile for the first time. Sure, it was only a brief moment. But it was a smile nonetheless, and he'd take it.

THE ROUNDS

Feeling a surge of confidence, Brian took on the other employees one by one.

With Patty and Jolene, he agreed with them that tips were a pretty good measure. But he also suggested that they count the number of unprompted customer comments about their service, either received by the waitresses directly or by one of the other employees. They agreed more easily than Brian had guessed, which he decided was a function of their gregarious personalities and the existence of a financial incentive for doing well.

Tristan's work at the cash register and on the phone was more difficult to measure, but after a few rejected suggestions, Brian and he agreed on three: the timeliness of turning around customer bills for waitresses, his creative ability to configure tables and get people seated, and the timeliness of answering the phone. The first two of these would be based, at least in part, on the judgments of Patty and Joleen.

Joaquin and Kenny in the kitchen were fairly easy. They would measure their success by the timeliness of finishing orders and the comments of customers about their food. In the latter case, they too would have to rely on the feedback of the waitresses, as the cooks had little or no direct contact with the people consuming the products they made.

Brian decided that Harrison, the driver, would not be measured on the timeliness of his deliveries because most of that was out of his control and more a matter of how fast the kitchen churned out an order. And Brian certainly didn't want him driving carelessly. Instead, Harrison's success should be measured in tips, order accuracy, and customer reaction, though he explained it differently to his burly, red-bearded renegade driver—someone who was sure to hate the idea of measuring smiles.

Salvador, the dishwasher, would be assessed based on having an adequate supply of dishes and utensils for the other employees, as well as the cleanliness of his product.

Migo was the most difficult to pin down because his job varied so much. He and Brian agreed that feedback from the other employees in the restaurant would be the best indicator of his success, and though Brian suggested that Migo solicit that feedback himself at the end of each night, the young man insisted that Brian do it, to ensure that the input from colleagues was honest.

By the end of the evening, everyone had identified how they would measure their own success, and some had even begun trying it out. While Brian could not say that they seemed exuberant about the new program, he honestly felt that there was a subtle sense of enthusiasm around it, which he attributed to more than just the additional wages.

As he locked up the restaurant that night, Brian was genuinely excited, eager to see his program put fully into practice the next Thursday.

COLD WATER

The car in the driveway at the cabin was unfamiliar to Brian, and on closer inspection, he could see it was a rental. When he opened the front door of his home, he was greeted with slightly forced smiles from Leslie and his daughter, Lynne.

Lynne had flown to the area to interview in South Lake Tahoe, but after a brief three-way call with her brothers, she'd added a second item to her agenda: check on dad's sanity.

After the usual greetings and hugs and small talk, the family sat down in the living room. Lynne, never one to back off from a challenge, broached the subject.

"So what's the deal with this job of yours, Dad?" She smiled, but in an almost sad kind of way.

Brian wasn't the least bit defensive. "Well, I'm sure your mother told you. I'm a part owner in a little Italian restaurant down the hill—you probably drove right by it on the way here—and I manage the place on Thursdays, Fridays, and Saturdays."

"And what made you do something crazy like that?"

Brian smiled, amused and proud of his daughter's protectiveness. "I know it looks," he searched for a word, "well, crazy is probably the best way to say it, I guess. But I have my reasons and I'm actually excited."

Lynne winced. "What are they paying you? Eight bucks an hour?"

Brian laughed. "Actually, they're not paying me at all. I'm an owner, and I decided to forgo the wages."

Leslie stepped in gently. "He's obviously not doing it for the money."

"I'm sorry to keep asking, Dad, but why exactly are you doing this?"

Brian proceeded to tell her about the difficulty of having his career end so abruptly, and about Rick Simpson's comments. He explained his general sense of frustration about the fact that so many people in the world hated their jobs, and how he felt like it might be the reason God put him on earth.

Just as he had been with is wife a week earlier, Brian was very compelling. Perhaps because she was looking for a job herself, or maybe because she tended to be empathic, Lynne seemed to be accepting and understanding what her dad was saying.

"So how long are you going to do this?"

Brian hesitated, as though he really hadn't given it much thought. "I don't know." He pondered the question. "Two months. Maybe six. Maybe a year."

Leslie squirmed. "A year? You don't really think you'll be down there that long, do you?"

"It depends on how long it takes me to figure it out."

"To figure what out?" Lynne wanted to know.

"How to help those people find some kind of fulfillment in their work. And why so many people with jobs like theirs are miserable."

"Okay, now I have to ask a question for Eric." Lynne went through her notes, to ensure that she quoted her brother accurately. "Here it is. Eric wanted me to ask you, 'Have you lost your mind, Dad?'"

They laughed at the blunt nature of the oldest son.

"You can tell Eric to stop worrying about me. I'm fine."

Lynne seemed satisfied for the moment, so the family shifted their focus away from Brian's work and onto her job interviews.

INITIAL RESULTS

Thursday night couldn't come quickly enough for Brian.

After reminding everyone before they left on Saturday night, Brian was glad to see that they all arrived on time. Unfortunately, the measurement part of his plan didn't go quite as well.

Some of the workers had already forgotten what they'd be measuring, while others seemed to have a hard time doing their jobs any differently than they had in the past. Brian reminded himself that these were not "A" players; some would have been stretching to merit a "C." The top waiters and waitresses and busboys and cooks in the area were working at nicer restaurants or hotels. He knew full well that Gene and Joe's was not employing the best and the brightest. Which only made Brian more determined to help them. And to be more patient.

By the middle of the Friday night shift, Brian had the measurement system working pretty well. He noticed that the waitresses were keeping a closer eye than usual on their tips, and that the guys in the kitchen were paying a little more attention to the time it took to get an order out. Carl wasn't having a great deal of luck making people smile, but he was more pleasant to customers than he had been the preceding week, and he was double-checking his orders before passing them through the window.

To different extents, everyone at Gene and Joe's seemed to be doing a little better. And by Saturday night, employees were checking out each other's scorecards at the end of the shift and comparing their respective results.

During the next weekend shift, the mood and performance at Gene and Joe's had begun to show signs of improvement in small but noticeable ways. Tips were getting a little bigger, errors were a little fewer, and the place even seemed a little cleaner. Brian was feeling like his experiment might be over sooner than he had expected.

More important, employees were spending more of their time at work talking about something they'd rarely discussed in the past. Work. They gave each other advice about how to get things done more quickly, and how to deal with customers in a way that would provoke a bigger tip or a humorous reaction.

But toward the end of Saturday night, as he was helping Migo, Tristan, and Carl close the place down, something happened that destroyed any sense of complacency Brian might have been feeling.

BLIP

Brian was closing out the cash register, while the rest of the crew were in the dining room cleaning tables, mopping the floor, and turning chairs over.

"Hey, Carl," Brian called out. "How many smiles you get tonight?"

Carl's response was the worst thing Brian could have heard. "I don't know."

"What do you mean, you don't know?"

Without bothering to pause from his mopping, the drive-thru clerk explained. "I forgot to keep track."

Brian, as well as the others in the dining room, was stunned. "You forgot?"

He shrugged. "I just don't see why it matters."

Before Brian could respond, Tristan did. "How about a dollar an hour, dude? Do you think I really care how fast I get the bills done? Just do it."

Carl nodded, and looked toward Brian. "Yeah, I'm sorry. I'll do it better next week." He looked back to Tristan and Migo. "Sorry about that."

Brian assured them all that the wage increase was not in jeopardy as long as Carl got back on track. But he also came to the disconcerting realization that his program was missing something, and that without it, was eventually going to fail.

Brian went home that night and racked his brain about what he and the other managers had done at JMJ to make people enjoy their work. In spite of all the accolades and attention they received as a great place to work, they had never been all that specific or purposeful. "We just treat people the way we'd like to be treated," was how he usually explained it during an awards dinner or a press interview.

Now, however, that wasn't enough. Brian needed to do some forensic analysis to figure out his theory. And preferably, before Thursday. Otherwise, he would begin to lose what little momentum he had.

Knowing that he would need help, Brian sent a host of e-mail messages to various former colleagues, some of whom were still working at JMJ. He asked his head of human resources, his VP of operations, and a few of his line managers in manufacturing if they would share their thoughts about what they believed were the key drivers of morale and productivity.

Over the course of the next few days, answers came trickling in, and Brian was excited to read them all. Though none seemed to have a complete or specifically accurate assessment, all together it gave Brian the insight he needed to take the next step at Gene and Joe's. And to recharge his own enthusiasm for what he was doing there.

REALITY CHECK

rian went into work early on Thursday, and was glad to find Joe there. The two straightened up the restaurant and then sat down to talk.

Joe began. "How's it going? You still glad you're here?"

Brian nodded. "Oh yeah. I'm enjoying it. How about you?"

"Well I've been here for more than thirty years, so I'm pretty used to it."

Brian laughed at Joe's dry and deceptively clever humor. "No, I mean how do you like having me here?"

"Well, you haven't burned the place down. And receipts are fine. From what I can see, everything's going okay."

At that moment, Salvador and Migo walked in the front door.

Joe looked at his watch as though it were broken. Then he returned to the conversation at hand. "How's your wife doing with all of this?"

"You know, she's actually gotten used to having a few nights of quiet time at home, reading and watching old movies. And during the week when it's not as crowded around the lake, we go driving or hiking. We even rented snowmobiles the other day and explored the hills above our cabin."

Joe smiled. "So what did you want to talk to me about?"

Again, the front door opened, and this time Tristan came in. Joe looked at his watch again, and turned back to Brian. "Did you change the time that people are supposed to come to work?"

Brian shook his head.

"What in the hell are they doing here, then?" he asked, motioning toward the kitchen where the three employees were already at work. "Don't tell me they're here early?"

Laughing, Brian explained. "I've got them on a little incentive program, and part of the deal is they have to be here on time."

"What's the incentive?" the majority owner wanted to know.

"That's what I wanted to talk to you about. I promised them that I'd pay them a dollar an hour more in wages for two months."

Joe looked surprised, even a little upset, so Brian clarified.

"Don't worry. It will come out of my check. I decided not to take any pay yet, not until I get things in order. And it's temporary. After that, we'll go back to normal." He paused before adding. "But I am looking for a way to have everyone share in some of the tips."

Joe was noticeably calmer now, but still a little on edge. "Well, there is no way the waitresses will let you do that, and frankly, I don't even want you to ask them. Not without talking to me."

Brian realized that he should have cleared the temporary pay increase with his business partner earlier. "You're right, Joe. I won't do anything else like that without checking with you first. I just figured that since I wasn't being paid, you would—"

Joe interrupted him. "That's okay. Don't worry about it. It sounds like everything's going well." He paused and watched the front door open again, and two more employees walk through. "Besides, if you've found a way to get these misfits to come to work early, then you must know what you're doing."

Brian hoped he was right.

ROUND TWO

Though the restaurant was now about to open, no customers had yet arrived. So Brian called a quick meeting. As soon as everyone was in the room except Joaquin, who had adjusted his schedule to arrive later on Thursdays, he began.

"Okay, everyone. I just want to let you know that we're going to be adding something to our list of things we measure."

People were already feeling pretty comfortable with Brian, and Tristan shouted from the counter where he was sitting. "Do we get another dollar an hour?"

Everyone laughed. Except Joe, who was just observing the scene.

"No. This one isn't about money, but it is related to measurement, too. It has to do with figuring out who you're working for."

Patty spoke next. "Are you going to reorganize things and give us different bosses?"

Brian shook his head. "No. Nothing like that. What I mean is that I want all of you here to figure out who is the beneficiary of your work."

Blank stares let Brian know that he might be using bigger words than were called for.

Migo raised his hand, and Brian acknowledged him.

"Is that like life insurance?"

Brian didn't smile, not wanting to discourage Migo's participation or appear condescending to his staff. "No, it has to do with how you make a difference in the life of someone other than yourself."

Migo followed with another question. "Like your family?"

"Not exactly. I'm thinking more about how you make a difference in the life of someone here at the restaurant. Like a customer. Or a coworker."

Kenny raised his hand but didn't wait to be called on. "Can you give us an example?"

"Sure. Let's start with an easy one. Joleen."

The attractive, outgoing young waitress stood up. "Hey, are you saying I'm easy?"

At first Brian thought she might have been upset. But before he could clarify himself, Joleen and most of the other employees broke out in laughter.

Brian smiled and shook his head. "Okay. Joleen is a waitress. Who does she serve and how does she make a difference in their lives?"

The question seemed so easy that no one responded right away. Finally, Tristan blurted out. "She helps customers by bringing them food."

Brian nodded, but with a wince on his face that indicated the answer wasn't quite sufficient. "Well, you're right that she helps customers. But is bringing them food the real way she makes a difference in their lives?"

Tristan and a few others nodded their heads.

"Well, what if she's sarcastic and rude to them, throws their food down on the table in a huff, and ignores them the rest of the time they're here."

"We go out of business and I lose my job." This time it was Salvador, the shy and diminutive dishwasher. Because of his thick accent and the rarity of his comments, the room burst out into laughter.

Brian smiled big, glad to see Salvador taking part. "Yes, you're right, Salvador. We probably would go out of business."

The dishwasher seemed genuinely glad to have his boss agree with him.

"But aside from that, how can Joleen or Patty make a real difference in the lives of customers?"

Now the room was quiet, but not in a confused way. They all seemed to be thinking about the question. Before they could answer, Brian asked it in a different way, directing the question at the waitresses now.

"Think about things you've done in the past that might have actually helped someone in a meaningful way."

After another moment of consideration, Patty raised her hand. Brian motioned to her and she started talking.

"A few months ago a mom came in here with four little kids. All boys. They were behaving badly. Nothing terrible, just typical brotherly rambunctiousness." Patty looked around the room, glad to have the floor. "After I brought their food to the table, her youngest boy reached up and pushed the pizza onto the floor. Luckily I had taken the time to take the pizza off the plate that came out of the oven and put it on a cool one, otherwise that little boy would have burned himself."

She paused, and Brian jumped in. "Okay, that's good. But what about—"

Patty cut him off. "Wait a second, sweetheart. I'm not finished. Changing the plates wasn't how I made a difference in her life, though I suppose it helped."

Brian was amusedly taken aback by the abrupt response from Patty, but he was glad that she was engaging in the discussion. "I'm sorry, Patty. Go ahead."

"Well, the pizza splatters on the floor, the boys start screaming, the lady looks like she's about to cry."

"What did you do?" Tristan wanted to know.

"First, I shushed those kids and told them that they weren't going to get any food if they didn't listen to their mama. They quieted down real fast. Then I assured that lady that we weren't going to charge her for the second pizza. And then I went to the kitchen and grabbed four hunks of pizza dough and gave it to the kids to play with."

Her coworkers all looked impressed, so Patty went on.

"The lady thanked me, but she still seemed pretty upset, and embarrassed. So I told her that her kids were no different from mine or anyone else's that came into the restaurant, and that she shouldn't feel bad. Then I poured her a beer, on the house."

Tristan started clapping. "Awesome."

Carl jumped in now. "Can you come to my house?"

Everyone laughed, and Brian continued.

"So Patty didn't just bring that lady food. She helped her get through a tough spot in her day. And while all situations aren't going to be that dramatic, I'd bet that we could find a way to help every customer, at least in some small way."

Joleen spoke up. "Yeah, sometimes I could swear that I can make an old man's day just by calling him sweetheart, or by saying 'God bless you' when he leaves. And I like to do it after they've paid and are on their way out the door so they don't think I'm just gunning for a bigger tip."

Brian was loving what he was hearing. "And you guys," he pointed toward Carl and Harrison, "even though the drive-thru window and home delivery is a little different, I think you can see how this would apply to you too."

Both of them nodded their agreement with muted enthusiasm, though Brian knew that Carl would come around with a little coaching.

Brian was thankful when Kenny raised his hand again and asked the big question. "What about the rest of us that don't deal with customers very much?"

Migo and Tristan and Salvador seemed to be waiting attentively for the answer.

Brian was ready. "Let's start with you, Salvador. Who is it that you help, and how do you make a difference in their lives?"

This was too much pressure for the dishwasher, who shrugged and shook his head.

"Come on, Salvador, you help all of us." It was Patty. "You make sure that customers have clean plates and silverware. You wash all the pots and pans for Joaquin and Kenny and whoever else is in there cooking. If you're not doing a good job, the rest of us are pretty much screwed."

Though Brian would have explained it more delicately, he appreciated Patty's enthusiasm, and the positive impact it had on Salvador, who seemed to be swelling with pride.

Instead of waiting for more questions, Brian moved to the other employees. "Kenny. Who do you impact, and how?"

Kenny didn't hesitate. "Well, I think we make a difference for customers who want good food."

"That's true. Anyone else have input for Kenny?"

"You make a difference for me." To everyone's surprise, it was Carl.

Kenny was a little confused, if not by the answer, then by the person saying it.

"Yeah, I mean, I can't get people their food fast if you don't turn stuff around for me. When you're cranking, I'm a lot less stressed out."

"Same for us, Ken," Joleen added. "No matter how sweet we are to a customer, it doesn't matter if their food takes twenty minutes or if it's cold. You and Joaquin are key for us. Just like you are, Tristan."

She turned toward the cashier and phone answerer and backup busboy. "When we need to get customers their bills fast, it's usually so we can get them out the door and open up tables for someone who's waiting. And when you figure out how we're going to get a party of fifteen people sitting together when we only have two tables available on different sides of the dining room, you're like a magician."

Tristan tried to brush off the compliment. "There is way too much love in this room right now. It's freaking me out."

Everyone laughed. Brian was pretty sure this was the most fun these people had ever had at work. "Okay, what about Migo?" At that moment the front door opened and four disheveled skiers came in, looking for dinner.

"Migo, you and I can talk about this later. Remember, I want everyone to keep track of your measurements tonight. We can't let that go."

And with that, everyone got to work.

GLITCH

Thursday and Friday night went fairly well, in terms of both business and measurements. Though some of the staff members were doing better against their measurements than others, only one of them gave Brian an immediate reason for concern.

Harrison wasn't in the restaurant as much as everyone else, and so Brian had to rely solely on him for reports of his measurements. What was strange about those reports were that they always seemed to be the same, with no accompanying stories or anecdotes.

On Saturday night, about halfway through the shift, Brian pulled Harrison aside during a lull in the delivery orders.

"How's the customer satisfaction thing going?" Again, Brian avoided using the word *smiles*.

Without even thinking about it, the driver responded. "Good. Real good."

"Anything specific?"

Harrison scratched his beard. "Uh, not much. Just a lot of happy customers. And I made a guy crack up tonight."

"How'd you do that?"

Harrison frowned. "I can't remember. I think I just said something funny."

Brian pushed a little. "How are tips?"

"About the same. Normal."

"That's too bad. Patty and Joleen are up this week. Carl too."

Harrison looked away. "Yeah. I guess it's different in delivery."

Brian took a breath, and decided to push a little. "Tell me the truth, Harrison. Do you really believe any of this stuff about making a difference in people's lives?"

Harrison looked his boss in the eye to see if he was serious, and when he decided he was, admitted, "Actually, I think it's ridiculous. I'm a friggin pizza delivery guy, driving a 1992 Chevy Impala. I think as long as people get the food they ordered, all is good. This ain't rocket science, and it sure ain't the center of my life."

Brian nodded, and asked with no hint of judgment. "Why do you do it, then?"

Harrison laughed. "Because they don't pay me to snowboard, and I couldn't get a job with the ski patrol."

Now Brian's demeanor changed a little. "Okay, Harrison. Here's the thing. I know that this restaurant and this job of yours is not the sexiest or most exciting thing in the world. But if you're going to be here, if you're going to be part of this, then you owe it to yourself and your coworkers, and your customers, to make the most of it."

Harrison wasn't being convinced. So Brian changed his approach.

"Listen. I understand where you're coming from. I know this sounds silly, and that it's just a way to make some money so you can pay the rent and have fun. I'm not going to force you to buy into all of this."

The delivery man looked at Brian again, relieved to be understood. Until he finished his thought.

"But I can't let you work here if you don't."

Harrison slowly nodded his head. "All right. I get it. I'll do better."

Brian didn't think he was completely on board yet, but he knew that it might take him some time to get there. He decided to give it another week to see if Harrison could come around. It didn't take that much time.

CONFRONTATION

Thursday night was surprisingly busy. The restaurant was buzzing with activity, and the staff seemed to be working a step or two faster than they had been a few weeks before.

And then the phone rang. Tristan answered, listened for a few seconds, and then handed it to Brian who was standing nearby, saying, "I think you need to handle this one, boss."

For the next five minutes Brian listened as a clearly irritated customer with a vaguely familiar voice complained about his order being late and not as hot as he wanted it. Brian apologized, assured him that he would have the cost of his food refunded.

Then he asked if he could speak with his driver to explain the arrangement.

"He took off five minutes ago."

Brian was confused. "He did? What did he say about all this?"

"Well, when I didn't give him a tip, he told me that it wasn't his fault, but that the guys in the kitchen were way behind. And then he told me I shouldn't punish him for other people's mistakes, and he left."

Brian assured the man that a coupon for a free pizza, as well as his refund, would be delivered to his door that night, and that he would do his best to make sure that nothing like this happened again. The customer, calmer now, told Brian that he didn't need a refund or a coupon, but thanked him for the thought.

Ten minutes later, Brian saw Harrison walking through the kitchen, having come in through the back door. Calling his driver over, Brian asked if they could have a word outside the building.

Brian didn't hesitate. "I just got a call from a guy on Beresford Place."

Harrison didn't even wait for him to finish. "Look, that guy was a jerk. The order was made a little too early so it was getting cold before I even picked it up. Then I got stuck in some casino traffic. The guy acted like the friggin world was coming to an end."

Brian couldn't believe what he was hearing. "You don't want this job, do you?"

"Yeah, I do. I just don't want to have to deal with people like that. I mean, the guy lives in a three-story mansion and can't tip me because his food is cold. Does he know what a microwave is? And does he have any idea how much money—"

Brian stopped the rant. "Harrison, do you have any idea what a tip is for?" He didn't wait for an answer. "Good service! We gave him a bad product and a bad attitude. That guy doesn't owe us anything. You're lucky he even paid the bill!"

"I don't care. He was a jerk."

"Well, you're going to have to go back there, refund his money, and give him a coupon. And I want him to call me and tell me how great we are for handling the problem this way, so that he orders food from us twice a week for the rest of his life."

Harrison shook his head. "No way. That guy stiffed me, and I'll be damned if I'm going to go treat him like he's more important than me."

Brian took a breath and tried his best to be calm, in an almost fatherly way. "He isn't more important than you, Harrison. He's just a customer. For all you know, he has a business too, and if you were an unhappy customer of his, he'd probably treat you the same way we're going to treat him."

"I highly doubt that."

"Well, be a bigger person than he is, then, and go make him a loyal customer."

"Sorry, dude. Can't do it."

"Then you can't work here, dude."

Harrison was momentarily stunned. "Fine. I'm out." And with that, he took off his jacket, removed his Gene and Joe's T-shirt, and threw it at the building. Walking away toward his car, bare-chested with his jacket on his arm, Harrison removed the magnetic signs from both doors and flung them to the ground. Then he drove off, screeching out of the parking lot, holding his hand out the window with the middle finger extended.

To his surprise, Brian could not keep himself from laughing. What he didn't know was that less than an hour later he'd be on the verge of tears.

STAND IN

Back inside the restaurant, a mini-crisis was in progress.

As he walked into the dining room, Brian could see a swarm of activity at one table in the corner. Migo was coming back toward the counter.

"What happened?"

"Little girl threw up her spaghetti all over table seven. I was walking by right when it happened."

"Tell me it wasn't food poisoning."

"Nah. The mom said she thinks she has the flu."

Brian was relieved, but suddenly found himself wondering why he didn't just buy a motor home and retire for real.

Coming to the front counter, he saw that Jolene was helping Patty deal with the mess and the melee, as Tristan headed for the bathroom.

"Where are you going?" Brian asked.

"I think I took some shrapnel in the bombing."

Brian was confused, so Tristan explained. "I've got vomit on my pants."

Brian couldn't help but laugh. Just then a call came from Kenny in the kitchen.

"Take-out orders twenty-two and twenty-three are ready to go!"

Normally, Brian would have asked Tristan to do it. But with everything going on, he didn't want to pull him out of the dining room and send him on a delivery. Especially not with pukey pants.

So he grabbed his jacket and headed for the kitchen. Grabbing a pizza and two bags of food, Brian left through the back door. "Tell Tristan and Migo I'll be back in . . ." he looked at the addresses stapled to the sides of the bags, "fifteen or twenty minutes."

Rounding up the door decals from the parking lot and putting them on his Explorer, Brian drove away.

SLAP

The first delivery was to a home just a half mile from the restaurant, in a lower-middle-class neighborhood away from the lake. Aside from a slobbery dog and a dark front porch, the transaction was quick and easy. Brian made a point to tell the older lady at the door that the latch on her gate was broken, making it easy for someone to get in or for the dog to get out. She seemed genuinely grateful for the warning.

The next order was further north, in a condominium complex. Brian made a wrong turn and had to stop and ask for directions, but found his customer, a young couple. After making them laugh by announcing that their Chinese food had arrived, Brian returned to his car to head back to the restaurant. He was no worse for the wear, and had earned himself a combined total of $5.50 in tips.

As he approached Gene and Joe's, Brian suddenly remembered the refund and coupon he had promised to the disgruntled customer earlier. He called the restaurant and asked Tristan for the address and the amount of the bill, and then continued south toward the upscale residential area above downtown South Lake Tahoe, about four miles away.

Harrison had accurately described the place. It was more like a mansion than a home, with three huge decks and a grand entrance facing a brick circular driveway. Brian pulled his car up near the front door and got out, leaving the engine running.

After ringing the doorbell, he turned and looked at the Gene and Joe's decals on the door. *What am I doing?* he laughed to himself.

Then he heard the lock clacking behind him, and turned to see a smartly dressed woman in her fifties open the door.

Before she could say anything, Brian explained. "Hi. I'm from Gene and Joe's. We fouled up your order earlier tonight, and I'm here to bring you a refund and a coupon for a pizza."

Before responding to Brian's offer, the woman turned and shouted to someone in another room. "Wiley, it's the delivery guy from that pizza place." Then she turned toward Brian. "I'll let my husband deal with this. Thanks."

Just a few seconds later the door opened wider and the man of the house emerged. "Hey, thanks for doing this, but you really didn't have to. I told the guy on the phone—"

Brian politely interrupted. "Yeah. That was me. I just wanted to say that we're sorry, and that—"

Now the customer interrupted. "Excuse me, do you have a brother?"

Brian was caught off guard. "Actually, I have three."

"You look just like a guy I know named Brian Bailey. You've got to be his brother."

And then it hit Brian. The man he was looking at was Wiley Nolan, one of the attorneys who had handled JMJ's product liability case during a public relations fiasco years earlier.

Brian smiled. "No. I'm not his brother. I'm him."

It took a second for Wiley to digest what he was hearing. "Brian?" Turning to his wife who was still standing beside him, he announced, "Honey, this is the CEO of that exercise equipment company that we defended years ago. What in the world are you doing delivering pizza?"

Brian did his best to act comfortable with the situation. In reality, he was pretty embarrassed. "Well, it's a long story, but the gist of it is that I sold the company, retired, and then got involved in a little restaurant, just to stay busy. It's kind of a project for me."

"Terrific." Wiley's reaction was a little too enthusiastic, and Brian felt the sting of his patronization.

Even Wiley's wife joined in. "I bet you're having fun."

"Actually, I'm having a great time. And learning a lot." Brian wanted to change the subject. "Hey, you don't still keep in touch with Rick Simpson, do you?"

Brian prayed Wiley would say no. He didn't.

"I sure do. In fact, I had lunch with Rick a few months ago, and I owe him a call."

Brian was desperate to get out of there now. "Well, I've got to get back to the store. It's great seeing you, Wiley," he turned toward his wife, "and meeting you."

"I'm Shirley."

"Shirley. Hey, my wife and I live in a place over near Evergreen Terrace. We should get together sometime."

"That would be great. This is our vacation home, but we're here at least once a month. Call us." Brian was pretty sure that she didn't mean it.

When the door shut, Brian went back to his car, pulled out of the driveway, and went down the road just far enough to be out of sight. Then he pulled over and rested his forehead on the steering wheel. "What in the world am I doing?" he mumbled to himself.

CONSOLATION

Later that night, after closing down the restaurant and calming down, Brian went home and explained his emotional state to Leslie.

"It wasn't so much that I felt humiliated. It was that they expected me to be humiliated. And I couldn't bring myself to explain to them what I was doing, and why."

"Why not?"

"I don't know. I suppose I wasn't sure they'd understand. And why should I care if they understand? I think there was a little part of me that was enjoying the simplicity of Gene and Joe's and the people there."

Leslie just listened.

"And then I run into these people, and out of nowhere they remind me of my other life. One without little girls throwing up spaghetti and underage kids trying to order beer with fake IDs, or shirtless men flipping me the bird."

"Who flipped you the bird?"

"Harrison, my delivery guy, but that's another story. Anyway, I think I just got caught off-guard tonight."

He paused, collecting himself. "And I have to admit that I'm not too excited about the fact that Wiley Nolan knows Rick Simpson. That's not going to be a fun conversation for me."

Leslie couldn't help herself now. "Well, you let me talk to that Rick Simpson, because I'm going to give him a piece of my mind. I still don't know why you bother ever talking to him."

Brian laughed.

"What's so funny?" Leslie wanted to know.

"You sound like my mother. Like I'm a fifth grader who's being picked on by a bully at school."

Both of them laughed and calmed down a bit.

Brian explained. "I think I'm just a little overwhelmed by what happened tonight. I'm fine. Besides, I've got bigger problems than Rick Simpson to worry about. I've got to find me a pizza delivery man."

He smiled and explained his ordeal with Harrison. Leslie hung on every word. Finally, exhausted and slightly amused by the unexpected state of their lives, the Baileys went to bed.

FRIDAY NIGHT HOOPS

Though he was now short a delivery guy, Brian went to work in a good mood the day after his encounter with Harrison. In fact, he was determined to get back out there and deliver again if that's what had to be done. Brian was on a mission and wouldn't let a little matter like pride or self-esteem keep him from finishing it.

Friday night started busy, and seemed to stay that way. Tristan and Brian shared responsibility for deliveries, though they were both glad that the order volume faded relatively early. The dining room was another story.

Joleen and Patty seemed to be sprinting back and forth to the kitchen all night, with Migo and Tristan diving in whenever they could. At eight o'clock, when it was usually starting to slow down, the place was still packed. But Brian had grown accustomed to the swings in business at Gene and Joe's. As quickly as the craziness started, it ended just as abruptly.

By 8:55, the only remaining table paid their bill and headed out. As the door closed behind them, the entire crew seemed to take a deep breath and sit down. Brian checked the receipts and discovered that it had been a good night for the restaurant. He looked forward to telling Joe.

And then something happened that would prove to be a test for Brian and his evolving staff. It came from Joaquin in the back.

"Autobus! Autobus!"

And with that, the chain reaction began. Tristan and Migo started flipping chairs. Carl hit the lights. Joleen and Patty cleared the last of the dishes from the tables by the door.

The bus pulled up close enough for the crew, who had already retreated to their corners, to see. Brian could feel their anxiety, and even empathize with them a little. He knew that this was a moment of truth.

As one of the parents hopped out of the bus, the staff members held their collective breaths. And that's when Brian made his move.

First he flipped on the dining room lights, to the horror of his employees. Then he went to the door, opened it, and waved the bus full of hungry basketball fans inside.

When he returned to the dining room, the crew was speechless. Brian took them on.

"Come on folks, we have a bus full of hungry customers out there. And if my judgment is correct, they lost tonight's game and they need some kindness. I know it's late, but this is what we do. So let's make the most out of this and have some fun."

Slowly, the staff emerged from their hiding places to prepare for the crowd that would fill the dining room. Though they were initially less than excited, as soon as the customers started coming inside, the mood changed. Within ten minutes, the dining room was as lively as it had been just an hour earlier, and the crew had regained their momentum. Brian was relieved. And proud.

By 10:15, the last of the Lakeview High School boosters club was gone, and the staff was looking at another thirty minutes of work before the place would be closed. That's when Brian had an idea.

Though any resentment they had felt for him earlier was gone, Brian wanted to do something to demonstrate his appreciation. Going to the kitchen, he packed up all of the extra food—a pizza and enough rigatoni with meat sauce to fill five orders, and left, saying, "I'll be right back." No one knew where he was headed, or why he had taken food with him.

Twenty minutes later, Brian returned, with two different kinds of bags in his hands. He went to one of the dining room tables and started unpacking them.

"Whatcha got there?" Joleen wanted to know.

"Food." Brian answered, without fanfare.

One by one, the rest of the dining room crew started to come by. "Go get the guys in the kitchen," Brian told Tristan. Within minutes, everyone was there, watching as Brian unloaded enough Chinese and Mexican food to feed, well, at least ten people.

It was as though the staff, who had been up to their elbows in pizza and pasta for the past six hours, hadn't eaten in weeks.

"Where'd you get this?" Migo asked.

"I went to Mandarin Palace and Pablitos and traded them some of our stuff for it. They were thrilled." Brian knew that the prospect of eating Italian food, especially the food they had to serve night after night, had no appeal to his employees. He figured, and rightly so, that the same held true for any other restaurant crew.

For the next forty-five minutes, Brian and his staff ate a bizarre combination of what they started calling "Chixican" food. With their manager's permission, they had complimentary beer and wine, though Brian was careful to see that no one had enough to impair their driving.

Conversation during dinner ranged from interesting customers they had that night, to Harrison's quitting, to the need for different kinds of beer in the restaurant. And probably because of the food that came from other kitchens, they talked about their experiences working in other restaurants.

This fascinated Brian, for a few reasons. First, even though most of them seemed to have been pretty miserable in their other restaurant jobs, they seemed resigned to the fact that they'd keep working in the industry.

Second, and more important for Brian, it was the first time that he could remember hearing them talk at any length about their lives outside Gene and Joe's. Aside from brief offhand comments about a girlfriend or a car problem or a movie that someone had seen, there had been relatively little self-disclosure, and certainly nothing terribly personal.

Though Brian couldn't be sure, he felt that this somehow factored into their job dissatisfaction. He was determined to find out how.

ANNIVERSARY

Monday night marked Brian's two-month anniversary at Gene and Joe's, and to celebrate the odd occasion, Leslie took her husband to dinner. Quickly deciding against Italian, Leslie suggested a Thai restaurant on the California side of South Lake Tahoe.

Brian promised not to talk about work, which reminded Leslie of their conversation in Napa. "Wow. Six months ago we were at Tra Vigne talking about your retirement over dinner."

"Was that just six months ago?"

Leslie smiled. "Yep. And if you'd have told me then that we'd be sitting here today celebrating your two-month anniversary of managing a slightly dumpy Italian restaurant, I'd have cried a lot more."

They laughed.

"I'm sorry, Les. I'm not much fun being married to, I'm afraid."

"Oh, quit it. You're an adventure, and I wouldn't trade it for anything."

They spent most of dinner talking about their kids, the cabin, and their next snowmobiling adventure. Finally, it was Leslie who broached the subject of work.

"So, how do you think things are going for you at the restaurant?"

"Well, revenue's up. Tips are up. I think this month is going to be huge."

Leslie smiled. "No. I mean how is your job misery experiment going?"

Shifting gears, Brian thought about it for a minute. "Well, I figure I'm about halfway toward figuring it out."

"You mean halfway in terms of time?"

"No. I'm not sure how long it's going to take. I mean in terms of rounding out the theory."

"I thought you said they seemed to be liking their jobs more."

"Yeah, I think so. But I don't know how long that will last, and whether it's just a function of having a new manager. For all I know, this is how it always is when someone new comes."

Leslie shook her head. "Give me a break. You think if you came in there and started being a jerk that they'd like their jobs more? You're smarter than that. Don't pretend that you're not making a difference."

"Okay. Okay. But I'm honestly concerned that it's not sustainable. I think something's missing still, and if I don't figure it out before I have to cut their wages back on Saturday, my window to prove this thing might close."

"Why don't you tell me about your theory?"

Brian took a breath and smiled. "I thought you'd never ask."

IMMEASUREMENT

As the couple ate their dessert, Brian dove in.

"Okay, I want you to push back on me if something doesn't sound right. Because I really need to be sure that this makes sense."

Leslie held up her hand as if to say *I promise.*

Brian began. "The first part of my theory I'm feeling pretty good about. Basically, a job is bound to be miserable if it doesn't involve measurement."

Leslie frowned. "Where'd you get that one?"

"Well, my grandfather taught it to me when I was a kid, and I've used it in every management job I've had."

Leslie had a mouthful of ice cream, but she motioned for her husband to continue. So Brian did. "He used to say that if you couldn't measure what you were doing, then you'd lose interest in it. And I think he was right."

Leslie swallowed and asked her first question. "I don't get the connection?"

"Well, if a person has no way of knowing if they're doing a good job, even if they're doing something they love, they get frustrated. Imagine playing a football game and not knowing the score. Or being a broker and not knowing if the price went up or down after you bought a stock."

"Does that really happen?"

"Well, not in those situations. But in most jobs it happens all the time."

"Give me an example." Leslie was a little more forceful than usual because of the promise she'd made.

"Okay." He thought about it. "Let's say Lynne takes that internship with the hotel in South Lake Tahoe, and they put her at the front desk."

Leslie liked it. "Go on."

"Every day she comes to work and checks people into the hotel, gets them their keys, takes their credit cards, and checks others out. People in, people out. That will be okay for a few days or weeks, as long as she's learning something new. After a while, though, it gets old. It's an endless cycle. There's no sense of progress."

"Sounds like being a mom. Laundry, dishes, cleaning."

"Yeah. But it's not just about monotony. It's about lack of feedback. "

"And that's the problem with being a mom sometimes. You don't get feedback."

Brian was nodding now. "Oh, right. I need to be clearer here. I'm not talking about feedback from a person, like an attaboy or attagirl. That's something else. I'm talking about objective evidence that tells you you're doing something right. Even supposedly exciting jobs get old when there's no way of measuring progress."

"I think I need another example."

Brian looked at the floor, thinking. "Okay. Think about Hollywood. You ever wonder why people in the movie business hate their jobs?"

"What do you mean? I thought everyone wanted to get a job in Hollywood?"

"Have you ever met someone who worked in that industry?"

Leslie thought about it, and shook her head. "Have you?"

"Sure. Remember Hunter Knox? He was in my high school class. He's a film editor now, and he's doing well. Making feature films. Anyway, I talked to him at our reunion a couple of years ago, and he told me that working down there is horrible. Everyone complains about it."

"Did he say why?"

"Yeah. He said it's all too subjective. Everything's based on someone's opinion, and most of the opinions are uninformed. There's no real sense of progress or achievement."

Leslie frowned. "What about box office receipts, or TV ratings, or Academy Awards?"

Brian shook his head. "I asked him the very same question, and he said that by the time you know what the ratings or ticket sales are, it's months and months after you've finished the project. And the awards take even longer, and even then they're based on total subjectivity."

"Well that explains the bizarre choices for Oscars and Emmys."

"But let's forget about Hollywood for a second, because it's really not about any particular industry. Whether you're a doctor, a lawyer, a janitor, or a game show host, if you don't get a daily sense of measurable accomplishment, you go home at night wondering if your day was worthwhile."

Things were starting to click for Leslie. "When I was teaching, I liked the test days. Even though most of the teachers hated doing it, I liked going home to grade the exams and the papers, because I wanted to know if the kids were learning what I was teaching them."

"Right. Otherwise, how do teachers know if they're succeeding?"

Leslie rolled her eyes. "Well, some of them used to say that as long as they were trying hard and they cared about the kids, they were doing a good job."

"I bet the best teachers didn't say that."

Leslie thought about it. "No. It was usually the bad ones who did. Why is that?"

"Because people who aren't good at their jobs don't want to be measured, because then they have to be accountable for something. Great employees love that kind of accountability. They crave it. Poor ones run away from it."

"Did employees at JMJ do a lot of measuring?"

Brian laughed. "Oh yeah. But they didn't measure everything. We didn't want them creating a bunch of bureaucratic tracking systems for every little activity. Did I ever tell you about ISO 9000?"

Leslie shook her head. "What was that?"

"Forget about it. It's a long, boring story and it was a waste of time because it was measurement for measurement's sake. The key at JMJ was always to measure the right things. If you measure the wrong things, people still lose interest."

"How do you know what the right things are?"

He smiled. "I think I figured that out last week."

IRRELEVANCE

Brian was getting more excited now. "The second cause of misery at work is irrelevance, the feeling that what you do has no impact on the lives of others."

"What does that have to do with measurement?"

"I'll get to that in a second. First, let me explain what I mean by relevance."

Leslie didn't let him. "You mean like a doctor caring for patients or a firefighter helping people get cats out of trees."

Brian forced himself to nod. "Those are some of the more obvious ones." Now he decided to turn the tables on Leslie and question her. "But what about all the other jobs? The unsexy ones. The car salesmen. The software programmers. The receptionists—"

She interrupted him, smiling. "The restaurant manager."

"Ouch." Brian laughed. "So how do they make a difference in the lives of others?"

Leslie thought about it, and answered as though she were taking a test. "Okay, the teacher's aide helps teach the children. The restaurant manager helps people get food for—"

Brian interrupted. "No, no, no. I'm not looking for a specific answer. Because there aren't any. It really depends on the situation and the job, and more than anything else, the person."

"Okay, you lost me."

"Yeah, I lost myself, too. Let's get back to basics. Every human being that works has to know that what they do matters to another human being. Not just in terms of bringing home a paycheck. I'm talking about the actual work they do. In some way, their work has to make a difference in someone else's life."

Leslie listened carefully, nodding her agreement, but with a perplexed, almost disappointed look on her face.

"What's wrong," Brian wanted to know.

"What do you mean?"

"I mean, you have a look on your face. Is this not making sense?"

She hesitated for a second. "No, no. It makes perfect sense." She winced. "It's just, I don't know. Don't take this the wrong way."

"I won't. Go ahead."

"Well, isn't this all just a bit obvious?"

To her surprise, Brian wasn't the slightest bit hurt by the comment. In fact, he came alive. "Absolutely! It's completely obvious!"

Leslie laughed at her wacky husband. "Why are you so excited?"

"Because as obvious as it is, no one does it! It's so ridiculously clear, and yet almost none of the managers out there take the time to help their people understand that their jobs matter to someone!"

Now Leslie decided to be difficult. "Isn't that the responsibility of the employee to figure that out?"

Brian's eyes went wide. He was incredulous. "Well, no, it's the manager's."

"I don't know." Leslie was doing her best job of acting now. "It seems to me that if employees can't do that for themselves, maybe they don't deserve to have that job in the first place."

Brian didn't know how to react. The look on his face said, *who is this awful woman?* Finally, he spoke, in a frustrated if not slightly judgmental tone. "Leslie, if a manager has any responsibility in the world, it's to help people understand why their work matters. If they don't think that's their role, then *they're* the ones who don't deserve their job. I mean, don't you think that every human being deserves to know how they make a difference in—"

Leslie started laughing, which brought Brian's tirade to a halt. "What's so funny?"

Through her laughter she explained. "I'm sorry. I was just teasing. I was trying to be tough."

It took Brian a second to adjust his disposition. "Oh. Okay." He smiled at his wife. "Then this makes sense?"

"Of course it makes sense. Who could argue with that? I just can't understand why every manager in the world doesn't already do it."

"Well, that's a good question. And it's got a few possible answers." Brian had certainly thought about this. "Some of them don't think the jobs of their employees, or their own jobs for that matter, are important. They grew up with the same low expectations of work that their parents and grandparents had. And they don't know any different."

Leslie could see that. "What else?"

"This is going to sound strange, but I think a lot of managers are embarrassed to talk to their people in these terms. It feels corny or juvenile or, I don't know, patronizing, to sit down with an adult and explain how to make a meaningful difference in the lives of others."

Now Leslie was thinking about something. "You know, even when I was teaching, and for that matter, volunteering at church, no one ever really talked to us about this kind of stuff. It was implied—but never really discussed seriously. And I honestly don't think people really saw themselves as making a difference."

She thought about the situation for a moment. "And I can't believe I'm going to say this, but I'm not sure the job satisfaction at school and at church was much higher than at your pizzeria."

Brian was popping out of his chair now. "That's the amazing thing. Professional football players, actors, CEOs, politicians. Everyone thinks those people love their jobs, but they're bound to be just as miserable as anyone else if they don't have a real sense of how their work is making a tangible difference in other people's lives. And based on the people I know in those fields, I don't think most of them do. I see lots of misery out there."

"Anything else?"

Brian was lost now. "Anything else what?"

"Any other reasons why managers don't do this?"

"Oh yeah. Right. I think there's one more, and it's a tricky one. I think managers are often afraid or ashamed to admit to their employees that they are the person whose life is most impacted."

Leslie was confused. "Whose life? The manager's?"

"Yeah. For some employees, the manager is the person whose life they impact. But managers don't want to admit it, because it makes them feel egotistical or elitist. So they pretend it's not true, which, ironically, only leaves the employees wondering if their work matters."

Leslie had an epiphany. "That's what happened to me in my first year as a teacher's aide. Emma Riley always said that my job was to help the students. And then she would feel bad about asking me to do so many things for her, and I would feel bad about not doing more directly with the students. When in fact, if she had just said, 'When you help me, it allows me to help the students, and that makes all the difference in the world,' that would have been fine with me."

Brian was nodding now. "I've got a young guy down at the restaurant like that. Migo."

"You seem to like him, don't you?"

"The kid's great. But his job is tough to nail down. He does anything and everything. Well, one day I realized that the person he helped the most was me, because I was usually the one asking him to do something. If it weren't for him, my job would be so much more stressful. So you know what I did?"

"What?"

"I told him. I said just that: 'Migo, if it weren't for you, my job would be so much more stressful. You make such a difference in my work every day, and that makes me a happier person.' Pretty much in those exact words."

"What did he do?"

"He smiled, thanked me for telling him, and started coming to work earlier and staying later and working harder than ever before. Which makes me want to remind him how great he is, which makes him work harder. It's a beautiful cycle, and it's all real."

Leslie was completely into the discussion now. "Okay, remind me about your theory again. Job misery is caused by lack of measurement—"

Brian corrected Leslie's description of his theory. "Well, I call it immeasurement, but that's right."

She smiled and mocked her husband gently. "Well I don't think immeasurement is really a word."

"Well, it is now," he countered.

They laughed and she continued. "Job misery is caused by immeasurement and," she paused, "what do you call the second one?"

"Irrelevance."

"Immeasurement and irrelevance. Did you ever explain how they're connected?"

"No. I didn't. It's pretty simple, though."

"All of this is pretty simple, isn't it?'

Brian breathed hard. "It's so simple it's frustrating. There are consultants running around out there trying to figure out how to give people more stock options or better 401(k) plans or more ergonomic chairs—all of which is fine—but until someone teaches managers how to figure out what to measure and why their jobs matter, it's not going to make much difference. It's really insane."

"Okay, okay. Enough about that, preacher boy. How are measurement and relevance related?"

"Here's how. People ought to think about measuring those things that make a difference to the person or people they serve. If you exist to help students, measure something related to that. If your purpose is to help your manager, find a way to measure that. If you deal directly with customers—"

"Measure it. Got it. Let's move on." Leslie was enjoying her role as the questioner. "Is that it? Immeasurement and irrelevance?"

"Well, until last week I thought so. But I think there's one more."

Silence.

"Well, are you going to tell me?"

Brian was now doing the acting. "Nah. I don't want to bore you. We can talk about it later."

Leslie knew when her husband was being coy. She picked up her knife and pointed it at him. "Oh, you're going to tell me, all right."

ANONYMITY

Brian wasn't joking completely when he said that he wasn't going to tell Leslie the third part of his evolving theory. "Let's not talk about it right now. Instead, let's go for a drive and I'll show it to you."

"What? Are you serious?"

He smiled. "Yeah. Trust me."

They paid their bill, got in the Explorer, and drove away from the lake for fifteen minutes before turning into the parking lot of what looked like a warehouse. A number of cars, not terribly nice ones, were parked around the building.

"What's this?" Leslie asked.

"You'll see."

They got out and went into the structure, which wasn't a warehouse at all but rather an arena of sorts, complete with artificial turf on the floor. On the "field" were twelve young men, mostly Hispanic, playing soccer. Sitting in bleachers three rows high were a collection of women and children and elderly people, alternating between watching the game and watching the kids.

"Brian, what are we doing here?" Leslie wanted to know, but not impatiently.

"You see that guy in the orange shirt? And the little guy in the yellow one?"

Leslie nodded.

"That's Migo and Salvador from the restaurant. They play in this indoor soccer league on Mondays."

"Does this have something to do with your theory?"

Brian nodded. "Yeah. It does."

At that moment Migo saw Brian and Leslie and waved.

Brian then explained to her what had happened on Saturday night when he brought food back to the staff and they stayed after hours. He told her that he started learning things about them that he wouldn't have imagined.

"What about the owner?"

"Joe knows next to nothing about these people. Most of them don't know a heck of a lot about one another. It's crazy for so many reasons. And don't you think that must have something to do with someone not liking their job?"

It was a rhetorical question, but Leslie indulged. "You mean wanting people to know what kind of person you are outside of work?"

"Basically, yeah. How can a person really feel good about going to work when they don't feel like anyone there knows who they are? Or cares?"

Leslie shifted back into her role as interrogator. "Well, I'm guessing that Migo and, what's the little guy's name?"

"Salvador."

"I'm guessing Migo and Salvador know each another pretty well."

Brian clarified. "Yeah, I guess it's really the person's manager who needs to know them. Coworkers too, but the manager has to be key. When I think back to the auto plant, it was Kathryn who made me love my job, and it was as much about her taking an interest in me as a person as it was anything specific she did connected to my work."

Leslie did her best to push back. "But isn't that a little touchy-feely? And aren't you supposed to keep your work life and your personal life separate? Why should a manager care what people do when they're not at work?"

"Because you shouldn't have to be a different person at work. That's part of what makes people miserable, pretending to be something or someone they're not. And that means their boss needs to know who they are beyond the job description alone. Les, can you see any justification for a manager not doing that?"

Leslie answered quickly. "Sure. Maybe the—"

Brian interrupted to clarify. "I'm not asking you to make up an answer just to push me here. I honestly want to know what you think."

Her demeanor changed immediately. "Oh, heck no. I don't think there is any excuse for a manager not getting to know the people who work for them. It's just part of being a good person."

They watched for a few minutes as Migo and Salvador's team gave up a goal.

Brian restarted the conversation. "Remember that great waiter kid at the diner? The one with the braces?"

Leslie nodded. "Yeah."

"Do you remember what his manager said when we asked about him?"

Leslie thought about it. "Yeah, he told us that he had just moved to town, that he was going to junior college, and had just gotten married."

"Do you think he knew his employees?"

Leslie nodded. "Did you know your people at JMJ?"

Brian thought about it. "Sure. I mean, not every single employee. But that's not really possible in a sizable company. The people I needed to know were those who worked directly for me, and others who I came in contact with fairly regularly. And somehow, just by doing that, I think we created a culture where others did the same."

"So I guess you didn't have this whole theory worked out back then."

Brian shook his head. "No way. We were winging it, other than the measurement thing. We just treated people like human beings. Human beings who wanted to be needed, and wanted to be known."

Leslie was shaking her head.

"What's wrong?"

"I just can't believe that with all of the money and technology and information that companies have, they don't do this simple stuff. It's crazy."

At that moment the whistle blew, and before he knew it, Migo and Salvador were jogging over to where Brian and Leslie were standing. "Hey boss," Salvador called out. "Is this your lady?"

Brian introduced them to Leslie, and then went over and met Migo's wife and children, and Salvador's brother. They talked about soccer, and the restaurant, and kids and Mexico for a half hour before saying good night.

As they were driving home, Leslie and Brian thought about Salvador and Migo and their families and how much they had learned about them in just thirty minutes. They were both surprised at how much education Migo had received before coming to the United States, and how someone studying to be an engineer could suddenly find himself chopping vegetables and busing tables in a roadside Italian restaurant, unnoticed. He was a diamond in the rough, and no one was even looking at him.

Leslie asked her final question of the evening. "Why do you think people like Joe don't get to know their employees?"

Brian thought about it. "Well, I shouldn't be too judgmental, because I've been there for two months and I haven't gotten to know them."

Leslie defended her husband. "But to be fair, you're only there on a temporary basis."

"Yeah, but that's not a good excuse."

Leslie continued her defense. "And you did know your people at JMJ. Stop being a martyr. I'm trying to figure this out."

He laughed. "Okay. I guess I don't know why Joe doesn't take time to get to know his people."

"I've got a theory." She paused before continuing. "I think most managers don't understand how *they're* relevant."

"Whoa. That sounds interesting. Tell me more."

Leslie continued. "Managers need to understand that the people whose lives they impact are their employees. And if they don't know who those people are, and what their lives are all about, how can they possibly do that?"

"I think you're right." Brian was quiet as he thought about it. "I think there's one more reason why they don't get to know their people. And I think it's the reason why I didn't do it."

"What?"

"It takes time. Managing people takes a lot of time. It's a full-time job, not something you do in between your regular work. Most managers don't see it that way. They see management as an extra activity, something you do when and if you have time. So the last thing they're going to do is sit down and talk to their staff about their lives."

"Or go watch them play indoor soccer."

Brian shrugged. "I guess so."

FULL STEAM

That night would mark a turning point in Brian's experiment, and in his career.

With his theory feeling somewhat complete, and with Leslie's full interest and support, he was now more committed than ever to getting his motley crew at Gene and Joe's to like their work. He hoped they'd give him enough time to pull it off. It certainly helped when Joe agreed to extend the wage increase another month.

Over the course of the next few weeks, Brian continued on his measurement and relevance plan, realizing that making it a habit required consistency over time. He also committed to taking an interest in his people and their lives.

But he was careful not to be disingenuous. Rather than interview them one by one, or ask them to fill out a questionnaire, Brian simply decided to become more human.

"These are people like you and me," he explained to Leslie—and himself—as he got ready for work on Thursday afternoon. "And if I can't find it within myself to know them as human beings, then I'm a hypocrite for saying I care about being a manager."

Here and there Brian began to make observations and ask questions. *How long have you lived in the Tahoe area? Where did you grow up? Where'd you get that tattoo, and why? What did you do for fun this week?* Here and there.

Soon enough, Brian was finding ways to demonstrate his commitment to knowing his people. If he saw a story in the paper about Mexico, he would take an extra few minutes to read it so he could discuss it with Salvador at work. When he learned that Patty's daughter was allergic to wheat, he worked with Joaquin to find gluten-free pizza dough for her.

He did other little things, nothing particularly indulgent. Whether it was bringing in a Michael Crichton book for Carl, who loved all things science fiction, or teasing Migo when his favorite Mexican soccer team lost a game to a rival, Brian merely wanted them to know that he was interested in them as people. And of course, he was.

When Salvador—who'd been there for two years—decided to leave the restaurant to move to Idaho with his brothers, Brian organized a special lunch for him to say good-bye. As modest as that lunch was, it turned out to be the first time that an employee's departure had been really acknowledged in any way other than Joe asking if anyone knew someone who could take their place.

And when Salvador's replacement and the new delivery driver started at the restaurant, Brian formally introduced them to the crew during a brief staff meeting, assigned a colleague to help them get adjusted during the first two weeks on the job, and promptly took them through "the program" around measurement and relevance, taking a little extra time with them to find out who they were and what made them tick.

RESULTS

Not long after adding the anonymity element to his theory, Brian watched as the momentum at Gene and Joe's began to accelerate. He decided that could not have occurred with just two of the three principles in play.

With no doubt in his mind that there was a new level of energy and commitment at the restaurant now, Brian felt that it was time to put some structure around his experiment so that any progress that had been made wouldn't slip away. So he created a simple spreadsheet, listing brief information about each of his employee's measurables, relevance, and personal interests. More important, he printed and carried the spreadsheet with him, reviewing it for five minutes every day before work, occasionally adding or modifying it as necessary.

As simple as that sheet might have been, over time Brian became convinced that it was key to turning things around at Gene and Joe's, both in terms of the level of job satisfaction among employees, and also—unsurprisingly—in terms of the financial performance of the business.

The increase in revenue over the past several weeks had been steady, and tips had skyrocketed. Beyond those two financial indicators, however, the energy in the tired Italian joint, among both customers and employees, was higher than it had been in years. Just as important, the crew was seeing more and more repeat customers, people everyone was coming to know by name.

When the time came for Brian to return the hourly wage to its previous level, Brian was confident that it wouldn't cause much of a problem. He was wrong.

MONEY

The employees who earned tips had no problem with the return to the old hourly wage. They were doing better than ever, and more than making up for it by inspiring customers to thank them generously for their service. The others in the restaurant were a different story.

During the short staff meeting when Brian reminded them of the need to readjust their salaries—with Joe on hand observing—it was Migo, of all people, who made the first comment. To be fair, his protest was calm, and as Brian would have to admit, reasonable.

"If Kenny's and Joaquin's job in the kitchen is to help Patty and Joleen, and they're making more tips and the restaurant's doing better, then shouldn't they get some of the reward for doing that?"

It was a question that Brian had no good explanation for. He was tempted to go into a long dissertation about the history of restaurants and the difference between a customer-facing employee and a cook or a dishwasher. Instead, he gave the only answer that he felt comfortable giving. "Yes."

The room was stunned. Migo had heard Joe fend off similar requests from the kitchen before, and he had friends at other restaurants who had unsuccessfully challenged the status quo. As a result, he and his comrades had come to accept their fate, that as long as they worked behind the scenes, their financial upside (though that's not what they called it) would be limited.

But with a new sheriff in town, Migo had decided it was worth another try.

Brian's answer certainly caught Joe off-guard, as he expected it would. But to keep the meeting from spinning out of control, and to ensure that the restaurant opened on time, Brian stopped short of making any promises that he couldn't keep. Not without the majority owner's permission.

"You make a good point, Migo. Let me think about this. I'm sure there's a way to do this right."

Again, the room was a little stunned.

Brian continued, deciding to be blunt. "But let me be clear. I don't want you guys losing sight of your measurables tonight because you're wondering what we're going to do."

He looked at Joleen and Patty. "Don't get caught up worrying that we're going to start pooling the tips and splitting them up among the whole restaurant. Because frankly, I don't think that's what we're going to do. What I do know is that if we keep making progress, all of us are going to be doing better. If we slip back to the old ways, we all lose." He paused to let that sink in. "Okay, let's get to work."

And with that, the room scattered. Joe asked Brian for a word in the back parking lot.

THE MAT

Joe wasn't overly angry, but he certainly wasn't pleased. "I hope you know what you're doing. Because this whole thing is probably going to blow up in our faces."

"You think so?"

Joe nodded emphatically. "This is a lightning rod in the restaurant business, and I don't want to touch it. Waitresses are coin operated, and if you go near their coins, they revolt."

"How do they do that?"

"First, they bitch like you've never heard. And then, after they've created a path of destruction like a tornado, they usually quit."

Brian nodded, thinking. Finally, he gently challenged his partner. "I don't think it's about money, Joe."

Joe's eyes went wide. "It's all about money, mister."

Brian was shaking his head now. "No, it's more than that. I mean, sure they want more money. Who can blame them? They live in a relatively expensive place and they earn relatively low wages. Anyone in their situation would naturally hope to make more money. I know that."

The look on Joe's face said exactly what was about to come out of his mouth. "No shit, Sherlock."

Brian laughed. "Yeah, that was brilliant, huh?"

Joe chuckled.

"But come on. A dollar an hour is not going to change their financial situation in any meaningful, or even noticeable way. It's not just the money. It's about feeling like they're being rewarded for their contribution."

Hesitantly, Joe could see a little logic there. In a tone that was somewhere between skepticism and sarcasm, he asked his business partner the big question. "So what do you suggest?"

"How about this?" Brian smiled. He was working without a script. "Let's let the kitchen crew and the other support staff keep the dollar an hour that I gave them before."

Joe winced, as he seemed to be adding up the numbers in his head. Brian didn't let up.

"And if the restaurant continues to improve, let's adjust it, up or down, every month. That protects you from a slump in the business, but lets them share in the success. Heck, it gives them an incentive to keep all this going."

Joe just sat there, peering at Brian and thinking about his proposition. Finally, he began to shake his head slowly. "I knew I shouldn't have hired you." And then he smiled. "Okay, let's try it for a few months on a temporary basis, and see how it goes."

Brian was pretty confident that it would work. What neither he nor Joe realized was that Brian wouldn't be there to find out.

THE CALL

I t happened at the beginning of a busy Thursday evening.

Tristan answered the phone and called Brian over. "It's for you, boss."

Brian came to the counter and took the phone. "This is Brian."

"I'd like to order a large pepperoni and anchovy pizza."

At first, Brian wondered why Tristan hadn't taken the order. And then the caller continued. "Do you guys deliver to San Francisco?"

It was Rick.

Brian did his best to be nonchalant and cheerful. "How in the world did you track me down here?"

"I talked to Leslie. She told me where to reach you." Rick paused, then laughed. "She also told me where I could go, if you know what I mean."

Brian laughed, more than a little curious. "What did she say?"

"Nothing that I wouldn't expect from a woman strong enough to put up with you."

Brian smiled. He couldn't wait to talk to Leslie.

Rick continued. "Anyway, I heard you were gainfully employed again, so I thought I would give you a call. How's it going? Sounds busy there."

For some reason, Brian did not like the fact that Rick Simpson could hear the restaurant noise behind him. Part of it was pride, certainly. The other was that he didn't want his sarcastic friend to enter into the world of Gene and Joe's.

"What can I do for you, Rick?" Brian was a little abrupt now.

"Well, I talked to Wiley Nolan yesterday, and when I heard what you were doing, I wanted to call to see if you had lost your mind."

Brian expected nothing less from Rick. In a completely serious tone he responded. "So Leslie didn't tell you?"

"Tell me what?"

"That I'm seeing a doctor and taking medication. He said it's something related to schizophrenia."

The line went silent. "Wow." Rick was at a loss. Embarrassed. "I had no idea, buddy."

Brian couldn't let it go on. "I'm pulling your leg, you knucklehead."

Rick laughed hard. "Okay. Well, you had me."

The restaurant was getting full and Brian needed to help Joleen move some tables to accommodate a big party in the dining room, and he wasn't exactly in the mood for Rick. "I'm fine. But I am busy right now. What do you need, Rick?"

"Well, I'm actually calling about business."

Brian was caught off-guard. "What do you mean? Something about JMJ?"

"No, other stuff. Why don't you call me when you have the time. I'll be home tonight, and I'll be up 'til midnight."

Brian told him he'd call when he got home, probably sometime before eleven, and hung up. For the rest of the night, he couldn't stop wondering what Rick might want from him.

THE BAIT

Brian drove the half mile home from the restaurant a little faster than normal. When he arrived, Leslie was already asleep. Desperately wanting to wake her to hear about her conversation with the infamous Rick Simpson, he decided against it and called Rick himself instead.

Disappointed when no one answered, Brian began leaving a message on the Simpson answering machine. "Hey Rick, returning your call on Thursday night. I'll be up for—"

And then Rick picked up the phone. "Hey buddy. Sorry about that. I couldn't find the cordless. How's it going?"

"Fine." Brian wasn't prepared for small talk.

"So, what's it like doing real work for a change? I was a cook in a seafood place in high school, and I waited tables in college. Sometimes I really miss doing that kind of work."

Brian was surprised at Rick's diplomacy, and let him continue. "But I have to tell you, working in a restaurant's a grind. Those people work their tails off."

Now Brian engaged. "They certainly do. I think that being a waitress for ten years would be like working in an office for thirty."

"Yeah, when my dad was out of work for a while, my mom waited tables. It crushed her. So tell me about your restaurant."

Disarmed by Rick's humble disclosure, Brian decided he had nothing to lose by opening up to the guy. So he described the whole Gene and Joe's story. How and why he had become a part owner. How he was trying to transform the staff and the culture in much the same way he did at JMJ. As usual, Rick couldn't resist a debate.

"Well, I'm not sure much can be done in that industry. But good luck."

"Actually," Brian countered, "I've already seen huge changes just by doing some of the things we did at the factory."

Rick continued to challenge him. "Well, it's one thing to do it in a little business where you don't have much vested interest in the operation."

Brian found himself getting frustrated again. "Well, I am part owner of the place. How can I be more vested than that?"

"Come on. What did you put in? Thirty thousand?"

"Twelve. But that's not the point."

"It is the point, Brian. Turning around a little operation as a hobby is not the same as having your reputation or career on the line. You know that."

Rick was being much more confrontational than usual. Gone was the subtle humor and clumsy teasing, replaced by plain old disagreeableness. Later Brian would kick himself for not seeing that his old friend had an ulterior motive.

Though he considered ending the conversation right there, Brian was too curious about why Rick had called. "Anyway, you said you wanted to talk business?"

"Yeah, I know you're semiretired and all. But I was just wondering if you might be open to a real opportunity I have."

HOOK

For the next hour, Rick laid out the details of the opportunity. It was a company, a little smaller than JMJ, that was looking for a CEO.

Desert Mountain Sports was a regional chain of twenty-four sporting goods stores sprinkled around Nevada, Idaho, Oregon, Utah, and Montana. It had been underperforming financially for the past five years in terms of both revenue and profit, and needed to be propped up for a while to make it attractive to a potential buyer.

Though Brian was more than intrigued by the idea, he knew that he couldn't even consider diving back into a full-time role, one that would require Leslie to move again so soon. But Rick was holding back two pieces of information that would change the equation drastically.

"You should know that the company's headquarters are in West Reno."

Brian didn't see that as being relevant. "Well I live in Lake Tahoe now, and I'm not going to—"

Rick interrupted. "It's eighteen miles from your house."

That was enough to stop Brian. For a moment.

"Look, Leslie is not going to want me going back to work like that. She's been more than patient with my situation at the restaurant—"

Rick interrupted again, this time to play his best card. "I already talked to Leslie about it. I think she's open to the idea."

Brian was dumbfounded. "You did what?"

"I mentioned it to Leslie earlier tonight. She and I had a nice talk. At least after she told me I was a jerk."

"She did?"

"Well, she didn't exactly use the word *jerk*. But that was the basic—"

Brian interrupted. "No, I mean, she said she would be open to the idea?"

Rick hesitated. "Well, don't quote me here, because I don't want to get back on her bad side. But yeah, she said it seemed like it might be something you'd enjoy. She did negotiate that you could work from your house one day a week, or spend it in one of our stores, which is in downtown South Lake Tahoe."

Brian didn't say anything, too overwhelmed by what he was hearing.

Rick continued. "Your wife certainly understands you, my friend. And for some reason, she seems to like you too."

Now Brian laughed. "Well, she's not going to like me when I wake her up. Let me talk to her and get back to you sometime in the next few days."

"Take your time. I don't have any other good candidates right now, anyway. No one I know is dumb enough to take the job."

They laughed and said good-bye.

PATIENCE

I n spite of his promise to Rick, Brian waited until morning to talk to Leslie, letting her sleep and giving him some time to think, and pray.

By morning, he came to a clear decision: whatever Leslie wanted him to do, he would do. Their conversation over breakfast was going to have a significant impact on the next few years of both of their lives.

"So you spoke with Rick Simpson last night." Brian was smiling, eager to hear what she had to say.

Leslie wiped the sleep from her eyes. "I'm guessing that means you did too."

He nodded. "So?"

"So the man is impossible to hate. I wanted to wring his neck, and then it occurred to me—the guy really cares about you."

Brian smiled and let his wife continue.

"I gave him a piece of my mind, though, and he took it like a man. He's a remarkably annoying and decent human being."

Brian laughed. "Yes, he is."

Leslie poured herself some coffee. "So what do you think of his offer?"

"That's my question for you!"

Leslie shook her head. "I asked first."

Brian smiled. "Okay, then. My decision is that you get to decide."

"That's not fair. You have to give me a real answer."

"That is my real answer. I am not going to do something that in any way diminishes this." He looked around the kitchen. "As much as I love solving problems, the thought of leaving you out, making you feel secondary, is not something I can handle. I'm not being nice here. I'm just telling you the truth."

Leslie wiped her eyes again, though this time not because of the sleep in them. She sat down at the table with her husband. "How long do you think it would last?"

"What? The assignment at the sporting goods company?"

She nodded.

"I want to err on the side of overestimating. So I'd say eighteen months, tops."

"What do you really think it will be?"

He had an answer ready. "Eight. Maybe nine."

Leslie took another drink from her coffee and asked the next question in a particularly serious tone. "So you think you could be available for next ski season?"

He thought about it. "Yeah, I think I can make that commitment."

Leslie reached out to shake her husband's hand. "Deal."

For the next hour, Brian worked out the conditions with his wife.

He would work from home at least one day per week, and limit his travel to Tuesdays through Thursdays, with occasional exceptions that she knew would occur.

But it was her last condition that surprised him most. "You can't just walk away from Gene and Joe's. You need to find a way to keep your experiment there working."

Brian was taken aback, pleasantly so, by the fact that Leslie would be so concerned about the restaurant. Or more specifically, the people there.

"I'm really glad you said that. I thought that I would continue to drop by the restaurant on Saturday nights for a while after I start at Desert Mountain, just to make sure that things are moving along."

Leslie asked the big question. "Who are you going to get to manage the place?"

Brian frowned. "I've been thinking about that for the last few hours. And the best answer I could come up with was, for right now, Joe. Eventually, I think Migo could do it."

Leslie raised her eyebrows, considering the idea. "Really?"

"Yeah. He's bright, educated, knows more about every aspect of the restaurant than anyone. And they respect him."

Leslie nodded. "That would be great. I hope it could work."

"Well, I'll have to start at Desert Mountain in less than three weeks. So it has to work."

HAND-OFF

For the next two weeks, Brian split his time between pushing hard for measurements and teaching Joe how to step in and fill the management role for a while. Joe proved to be his bigger challenge.

With more than thirty years of ingrained distrust of employees, Joe was having a hard time seeing his role as being anything more than keeping the inmates from running the asylum. Brian had to convince him that the inmates were actually quite sane, and that they really wanted the asylum to work.

The two assets that Brian had, which would ultimately get Joe to convert to his way of thinking, were the financial results of the restaurant during the last few weeks, as well as the imminence of his own departure.

They had a few difficult conversations along the way.

"Come on, Joe. You've seen it yourself. They're coming to work on time, if not early. They're helping each other close down the restaurant at night, instead of scattering like sixth graders heading for recess when the bell rings. Customers are happier. Revenue is stronger. What in the world do you have to lose by changing your mind here?"

Joe looked around the place. "Listen, I've been here almost half my life, and you've been here for ninety days. I think I have a little more at stake here."

Brian remained calm. "Okay, but how are you going to feel when it all goes back to the way it was?"

Joe looked just slightly hurt, so Brian corrected himself. "What I mean is, these people are excited about Gene and Joe's now, and they're getting something out of work beyond their eleven bucks an hour."

That's when it hit Brian. What was Joe getting out of it?

"You know what? I think you need to be part of the program."

Joe looked confused.

"How do you measure your success, Joe? And whose life do you impact?"

"Come on. Don't try that stuff on me."

"Stuff?" Brian was just slightly offended. "You think this is some touchy-feely hocus pocus? You don't think you need it?"

Joe shrugged.

"Give me fifteen minutes of open-mindedness here, Joe. Fifteen minutes."

Slowly, the owner nodded his head.

"Tell me first who you think you serve? Whose life do you impact here?"

"Brian, I'll go along with this, but don't make me answer the questions. Just tell me what you think."

Brian agreed. "Okay, I'll tell you whose lives you impact. And I think you already know the answer. These employees depend on their jobs for more than you know. Sure, they get their paychecks here, and that isn't something you or I can take lightly. But they get a sense of accomplishment, self-esteem, sanity, and community here too."

Joe was trying his best to remain skeptical, but Brian wasn't about to let him.

"As long as you think you've hired a bunch of misfits who don't want to be here and will only do what they're required to do, then that's what you'll get." Brian decided that Joe needed some tough love now, so he gave it to him. "And that's all you've been getting for years. And now you have a chance to change things, to be something real to these people, and wake up a business that's been asleep for years. It's up to you, Joe. It really is."

Joe got up from the table and poured himself a cup of coffee. When he came back to the table, he said, "Has it been fifteen minutes yet?"

Brian, clearly frustrated, shook his head. "I don't know."

"Because I thought maybe we should talk about how I'm going to go about measuring all of this stuff."

Brian smiled, pulled a napkin out of the dispenser on the table, and got to work.

Ninety minutes later, the co-owners of the restaurant had agreed that the four measurements would be nightly receipts, tips, return business, and employee satisfaction. Some would be easy to measure, others would require a little qualitative assessment and feedback. But they would form the basis for Joe's job, and his ongoing training of Brian's successor, Migo.

REORIENTATION

As the time for Brian to start his new job approached, he slowly began to move more and more of his responsibilities back over to Joe and Migo. During his last week at the restaurant, he stepped out of the nightly operations for longer and longer chunks of time, so that his absence the following week wouldn't seem so stark.

On his final night, the staff stayed a little late, and Joaquin brought in a small cake he had made, with the words "Adios Brian" written across the top. Though the occasion was certainly far less emotional than his farewell at JMJ, Brian was surprised at how attached he had become to Joe's motley crew in such a short period.

He addressed the staff briefly. "Okay, I want you all to remember that I'm a part owner in this place, so I'll be stopping by from time to time to check on your measurements. And I'll be ordering food for take-out using a fake name or coming through the drive-thru in disguise, just to make sure you're not running the place into the ground."

They laughed.

As he went home that night, any sadness Brian had been feeling was quickly overridden by his excitement about starting his next assignment.

PART FOUR

❖

Going
Live

TURNAROUND

Desert Mountain Sports was an underperforming medium-sized company trying its best, it seemed, to become a small one. As the sporting goods market was consolidating—something Brian was all too familiar with—few suitors were lining up to acquire the Reno-based chain. The only offers the DMS board had received were embarrassingly low.

As Rick Simpson became more and more frustrated at his inability to generate interest in DMS, he came to the conclusion that the company needed to be cleaned up before it would be attractive. "Let's put some lipstick on this pig," he said on more than one occasion, eliciting a pained laugh from his clients.

Though Brian had done significantly more research on DMS than he had before joining Gene and Joe's, no amount of diligence can prepare an incoming CEO for reality. There is just something about becoming an insider that brings with it a whole new perspective.

At his first board meeting, Brian learned that the headcount at the company's Reno headquarters was larger than he had been led to believe. Rather than the thirty-five he had expected, there were actually fifty-five people sitting in the glass building with a view of the city below. "I don't want to jump to any conclusions," Brian explained to the board that day, "but it seems a little excessive to me that we have twice as many employees here at headquarters as we do stores."

Heads around the table nodded agreement, as though they had not been part of the oversight, or lack thereof, that had created the problem in the first place.

But a closer look into the financials convinced Brian that cutting or moving jobs was not going to solve the company's problems. Brian had to find a way to increase revenue before he could persuade potential investors to lift a hand. If that didn't happen, all those jobs were bound to be cut anyway, by whomever was willing to take on the lethargic company.

After a series of meetings with his new staff and various senior employees, Brian learned why Rick had recommended the job to him in the first place, aside from the company's proximity to Lake Tahoe.

First, it had a customer service problem. An outside research firm hired by the board had found that Desert Mountain ranked eighth out of eleven sporting goods companies in the western part of the country. Second, and certainly related to the customer issue, it had a problem with employees. Too many were quitting, and the ones who stayed were either unmotivated or untrained.

That news would have been depressing to most CEOs, but to Brian, it was music to his ears.

RECON

After a series of meetings with his direct reports and other staff members at headquarters, Brian eagerly boarded a plane—his first since retiring—for a visit to a few of his largest stores, scattered around the West. Though he valued market research, he wanted to go out and verify that what he had been told was accurate and complete.

Brian was most eager to meet store managers, referred to as GMs, so he could begin thinking about implementing a program similar to the one he'd set up at the restaurant. But what he encountered would make that more difficult than he had imagined.

Ironically, the quality of the half dozen GMs he met greatly exceeded his expectations. At least on paper. They were all college-educated, professional, and had fairly impressive backgrounds. It was their level of enthusiasm that disturbed him.

Though they tried to put on their best face for the new CEO, most of the GMs were fairly open about their levels of frustration and burnout. Unsurprisingly, the employees who worked for them were just as unmotivated, if not more so.

Finding good employees to staff those stores was one of the biggest complaints that Brian heard from the GMs. The guy who ran the Boise store explained the prevailing wisdom best. "It's just hard to find a capable young person—or a retired one either—who is willing to work for ten bucks an hour these days. Either they don't need the money, or they need to make a lot more of it to support their family." He paused. "Or they aren't smart enough to work a cash register."

Another GM, this one in Reno, explained her dilemma. "I spend so much of my time recruiting and hiring, and then as soon as I think I'm all set, someone else leaves and I'm back out there working the register again. Between that and all the weekly reports I'm doing, I have no time to think about sales and marketing. I'm just keeping my head above water."

When Brian asked the GMs why employees were leaving, the answers he received were vague and unconvincing. The Reno GM blamed low pay, though Brian later learned that competitors were paying wages no higher than Desert Mountain, and sometimes lower. The Eugene GM claimed that there wasn't enough opportunity for career advancement. Still another, in Las Vegas, lamented that the school system just wasn't producing enough qualified young people.

Brian wasn't buying any of it. While it was true that some of DMS's competitors had similar turnover problems, others didn't. And those that didn't, as Brian had expected, tended to be the best financial performers.

During his trip, Brian spent hours with each GM, and plenty of time walking the floors of their stores talking to employees. And he personally surveyed more than a handful of customers as they were leaving each of the stores he visited. Wanting to separate problems unique to DMS from those in the industry at large, Brian also stopped by as many of his competitors' stores as possible, and he spoke to their customers too.

By the time he returned from his whirlwind trip, Brian began formulating a plan for what he would do to revive his struggling company. Unsurprisingly, much of his plan was centered around what he had done at the restaurant, which caused him more than a little concern.

HOME FRONT

When her husband came home from the airport, Leslie was up waiting for him. She couldn't wipe the smile off her face.

Before Brian could say hello, she blurted out: "Lynne got the internship in Tahoe! She's going to be staying with us through the summer!"

Suddenly, any of Brian's concerns about work were gone. Not only was he ecstatic about the thought of having his daughter home for the spring, he was relieved to know that his wife would have company if he needed to travel.

And what Leslie said to him next would give him the confidence that he needed. "And you know why she took the Tahoe job, don't you?"

Brian looked confused. "Well, I'm guessing it had something to do with us living up here."

Leslie shook her head. "Not really. I'm sure that didn't hurt, but it was the way she compared the various offers she received."

Still, Brian seemed confused, so his wife stopped being coy.

"Basically, she assessed how they stacked up against relevance and measurement and the anonymity thing. Not exactly in those words, but that's basically how she explained it to me."

Though he did his best to hide it, Brian was blown away by the fact that his daughter had remembered his theory after so little explanation from him. He was also more than a little pleased that she had used it to avoid finding herself in a miserable job.

After he and Leslie finished figuring out which bedroom their daughter would use, and what they would need to do to prepare for her arrival, Leslie shifted her focus back to Brian.

"So, tell me about your trip."

Brian told her about the GMs, the employees, the stores, the customers. He was strangely subdued.

"What's wrong?" Leslie asked.

"I don't know. I'm just a little worried about something."

"At work?"

"Yeah. It's the whole job misery thing."

"What's the problem?"

"I don't know. I guess I'm kind of worried that I'm going to be force-fitting my theory where it doesn't belong."

Leslie frowned. "I don't get it."

"You know that saying, 'When your only tool is a hammer, everything looks like a nail'?"

She nodded.

"Maybe the theory isn't for everyone. Maybe I'm seeing too many nails."

Leslie thought about it. "I don't think so. No way."

"You sound pretty sure."

"I'm certain. Come on, Brian. Why in the world wouldn't it apply to a sporting goods store? Or any other kind of company, for that matter? And why would any human being be immune to those things? I don't care if you're the Queen of England or a rock star, if you can't measure what you're doing, if you don't think it matters to anyone, and if you feel like no one is interested in who you are, you're going to be miserable at work."

Brian squinted. "You're not just saying that to make me feel better, are you?"

"Well, even if I didn't believe it I'd probably say it just to make you feel better." She smiled. "But in this case, no. I'm convinced. And you should be too."

Leslie could see that her husband was listening to her. "Now let's go to bed. We've got to get up early and go snow-mobiling."

DRIVE BY

Late Saturday afternoon, Brian couldn't wait to get down to the restaurant. Which, in itself, amazed him.

As he explained to Leslie on the way home from snow-mobiling, "I can't believe that I'm so excited about seeing everyone at Gene and Joe's. Who'd have thought?"

Leslie raised her hand. "I would have. It doesn't surprise me a bit."

"You mean you could have guessed that I'd be doing this? Come on."

"No, I'm still shocked that you took a job at a restaurant. What doesn't surprise me is how much you like the people there."

"Really?"

"Really. That's what I love about you."

"Well, I hope you still love that about me when I come home late tonight."

By the time Brian arrived at Gene and Joe's, everyone there was preparing to open the place. Though it had been just a week since his last time in the restaurant, the staff greeted him like it had been months.

As much as he enjoyed the informal interchange with the crew, Brian couldn't wait to hear how things were going with the business. He started by sitting down with Joe.

"So, how's everything working out? You're not going to quit on me, are you?"

"You think I'd be wearing this T-shirt if I were going to quit?"

They laughed.

"Things are going pretty well. I've had a few moments here and there, but I'm sticking to the whole measurement thing, and getting used to the fact that my customers are these knuckleheads who work here." Though the words he used were the same, Brian was certain that Joe now meant it in a largely affectionate way.

When asked specifically about how he was taking a greater interest in his employees as people, Joe seemed a little frustrated. "To be honest, it's harder than I thought."

Brian braced himself for a feeble excuse but was pleasantly surprised when Joe explained.

"They're all so interested in one another that it's hard for me to break in. Between Joleen and Patty and Migo giving people advice and attention, I'm really not sure they need any of it from me."

Brian assured Joe that they did and encouraged him to keep trying. He was relieved, and admittedly surprised, to know that his former employees were taking it on themselves to create a culture that would probably survive even if Joe struggled to catch on right away.

Brian went on to talk to various members of the crew, mainly to find out how their measurements were going and what was new in their lives. He decided to spend most of his time, though, with Migo.

"How's Joe doing?" Brian asked pointedly.

Migo hesitated, as though he were being asked to rat out a superior.

Brian clarified. "It's okay to tell me, Migo. This is so I can help him, and you. You're not doing anything wrong by talking to me about this."

A little more relaxed now, Migo explained. "He's kind of different than he was before. He's working harder, and pushing everyone around the measurement stuff, and being a little nicer and more involved with people."

Brian was glad to hear that. "How about with you? Is he spending any time teaching you the business?"

Migo initially nodded, though Brian could see he was uncertain. "Yeah, he tries to give me advice here and there."

Brian hadn't yet explained his plans for Migo, but decided this was as good a time as any. "So are you going to be ready to be the manager of this place in a few months?"

A look of mild surprise came across Migo's face. "Me?"

"Yeah, you."

Migo shrugged. "I don't know." He paused. "Do you think so?"

Brian nodded without hesitation. "Absolutely."

Later in the evening, as the crowd dwindled and the restaurant got more under control, Brian took Migo for a drive. They went to the Mountain Express, the place where Leslie and Brian had gone after his first night at Gene and Joe's.

Before going inside, Brian asked Migo to observe as much as he could, both good and bad, about the way the restaurant was run.

For the next ninety minutes, they watched, ate pie, drank coffee, and talked. And took notes about everything: the configuration of the restaurant, the way the food was presented, the menu, the processing of credit cards. And of course, the service.

Most of what he saw at the restaurant was pretty good, Migo said, but he went on to point out a few areas where improvements were necessary. Brian found these observations interesting and perceptive, but what he really wanted to see was whether Migo was curious about what was going on and holistic enough in his thinking to see the business beyond the details. On both counts, it was clear to Brian that Migo was on track.

Then Brian asked a question that Migo hadn't expected, but that was important for him to consider. "How do you feel about managing your manager?"

Migo didn't seem to understand. "You mean Joe?"

Brian nodded and explained. "I don't mean manage him as an employee. I mean, manage his behavior. You're going to have to guide him a little, keep him focused on the right things. And that means you might have to challenge him sometimes." Brian wasn't looking for an answer from Migo, so he continued. "The thing you have to realize about Joe is that he'll let you do pretty much anything you think needs to be done—as long as you're confident and he believes it will help the restaurant. You just can't be intimidated by him because he's the owner."

After a few more minutes of conversation, Brian and Migo left Mountain Express and drove back to Gene and Joe's, which was already closed down. They went inside, and sat down in the empty dining room.

"So, what do you think?" Brian asked.

"About what?"

"About managing this place."

Migo looked around for a few long seconds. "I think I could do it."

The smile on his face told Brian that he meant it. Both of them would look back on that night as a crucial moment for the restaurant, as well as for Migo personally. For Brian, it would alleviate some of his guilt for having to shift even more of his focus to Desert Mountain.

THE REPORT

On Tuesday morning, Brian called a special meeting of his direct reports to give them his assessment of what he had learned during his trip. At ten o'clock, almost the entire executive team was seated around the table in the company's main conference room: the CFO, two of the three regional vice presidents responsible for the stores, and the VPs in charge of customer service, merchandising, and human resources.

Even though this was just his third time with the group—and his first opportunity to really run a meeting—Brian decided to go for broke.

"I'm a believer that first impressions are sometimes your best ones. And so, after spending most of last week out in the field, and having quite a few in-depth conversations with all of you, I thought I should tell you what I think I see out there as soon as possible, before I get completely acclimated here and lose my sense of perspective."

The executives seemed a little less curious than Brian would have liked.

"Please challenge me or ask me questions. My observations and conclusions are based on conversations I had with six GMs, a few dozen employees, and about that many customers. I don't know that everything I'm about to say is correct." He paused. "But I'm guessing it's pretty close."

At that moment, the third regional VP came in, apparently unconcerned about being late. Rather than address the issue there, Brian decided to simply acknowledge him—"good morning, Rob"—to let him know he noticed his entrance. Then he dove in.

"Okay, let me start with a few of the things that surprised me. First, the GMs I met were more," he paused, searching for the right word, "*qualified* than I had anticipated. They're experienced. They know their products. And they're pretty good financially."

Some of the executives in the room nodded their heads, but most seemed surprised by the assessment. Finally, one of the regional guys, a short, muscular guy named Lou, spoke up. "I guess you didn't visit any of my stores."

The rest of the room chuckled. Brian smiled politely and continued.

"The other thing that surprised me was the quality of our competitors. Or I should say, lack of quality. Given the amount of market share they've been taking from us, and their better financial performance, I was expecting their stores to be bigger and nicer than ours, and their product selection to be greater. But that wasn't the case at all."

The men and women in the room seemed unsure about whether they should be proud or ashamed.

"What I wasn't surprised by, given the reports I've seen and the conversations I've had with you all, was the," again, he chose his word carefully, "behavior of the employees in many of our stores. As some of you told me, they seemed generally passive and uninformed."

"Maybe you *did* visit my stores." It was Lou again, but this time it prompted a heartier laugh, even from Brian.

"And so, the conclusion I've come to is that Desert Mountain Sports has a management problem."

Heads around the table nodded at the generic term. They wouldn't be nodding for long.

"That means we've got some training to do." Brian waited for a reaction.

After an awkward pause, his CFO, a well-dressed woman in her late forties, raised her hand but started speaking immediately. "I don't know if you're aware of the fact that we did a ton of manager training for GMs last year. And you said yourself, the GMs know their businesses. I spent two days with them myself explaining pricing and cost accounting, and they're doing well."

Brian didn't want to discourage dissent by disagreeing too quickly. He paused, hoping that someone else might have something to say.

The head of human resources raised her hand and waited for Brian to acknowledge her. "Yes, Suzanne?"

"Six months ago we did a comprehensive training program, part classroom and part online. We covered performance reviews, effective communication, and interviewing. Every GM went through it, and I just don't know that they're going to get a whole lot better with more training."

She hesitated before continuing. "I think we just have an employment problem. There's a shortage of good people out there. Recruiting is a nightmare."

Brian waited for her to finish, and took a moment to think about what he was going to say. "Suzanne, I'm going to have to disagree with you. I don't think that we have a shortage of good people."

She gently challenged him. "But you said just a minute ago that the quality of our employees was poor."

"No," he explained. "I said their behavior was poor. The people we're hiring are fine. They're no different from our competitors' employees."

Most of the executives at the table seemed confused, and Brian felt them collectively wondering if he knew what he was talking about.

"They're just not being managed well. And that's because their managers aren't being managed well."

It took the group of executives a moment to realize that he was talking about them.

The third regional vice president, a man about the same age as Brian, spoke first. "Excuse me, Brian. I don't want to sound defensive, but you did say you wanted us to challenge you if we thought you were wrong about something."

Brian nodded. "Absolutely. Fire away, Frank."

"Okay, it just seems like you're coming to some pretty specific conclusions after relatively little time with the company. Can you really have a high degree of confidence, after just nine days on the job, that we're bad at managing our people?"

Brian shook his head. "No, I can't, Frank. But my confidence is not based solely on my observations of DMS over the past two weeks. It's based on the fact that the vast majority of companies out there are really bad at management. And I don't need to spend six months pumping up soccer balls in Vegas or selling shoes in Eugene to verify that we are too. Our GMs out there are just as lost and miserable as their employees are."

The room took a moment to digest the new CEO's stark but compelling sermon.

"So what do you want us to do?" It was Rob.

"I want you to go through management training."

Brian wasn't at all surprised to see a few of his staff members roll their eyes.

The head of merchandising, a big guy named Spencer, spoke for the first time. "I don't know when we're going to be able to do any training before the end of the quarter. I mean, we've got trade shows next week and an Asian purchasing trip to get ready for next month."

Kelly, the CFO, joined in. "And we're going to be pushed to get the books closed on time. This is a crazy time of year, Brian."

Suzanne then asked, "When do you want to have this done by?"

Brian looked at his watch. "How about before lunch?

TEACHING TO FISH

For the next twenty minutes, Brian laid out his theory about job misery. He started with anonymity this time, then covered irrelevance, and finally, immeasurement. When he was finished, he had plenty of questions to answer and resistance to overcome.

Spencer went first, in a slightly sarcastic tone. "Let me get this straight. You're saying that we have to get to know our GMs better as people, tell them that they make a difference in someone's life, and then hold their hands while they come up with a way to measure their success?"

Brian laughed. "Well, you make it sound a little more preschoolish than I was thinking, but yeah, that's pretty much it."

The rest of the room was stunned. Brian verbalized what they were thinking.

"So, at this point you're all wondering where the board of directors found me, and how long it's going to take you to find another job."

The room laughed louder than Brian thought they would, which he attributed to the accuracy of his statement. As humorous as it was, it was also a little disconcerting. Brian decided he had to keep pushing.

"What did you guys think I was going to do? Come in here and tell you how to market sporting goods? Or give you a pricing strategy that would somehow spur sales without cutting into our profits?"

It was meant as a rhetorical question, but Rob answered it anyway. "Yeah, I was kind of hoping for that."

A few of the others laughed.

Brian smiled and shook his head in disbelief. "So, you're telling me that the problem at Desert Mountain is that the people in this room don't know their own market well enough. Is that it? You need someone to come in here with more intelligence than you and tell you how to run this business? Because if that's the case, we are all in big trouble."

The executives glanced at one another. Brian knew what he was doing.

"Well, no one is going to be able to do that for you. From what I can tell, there is no shortage of intellectual ability or industry knowledge in this room, and yet we're still struggling. I guess that leaves us with two choices. We can either throw in the towel and start looking for our next jobs. Or we can listen to this crazy new CEO who wants us to make our employees' work lives a little more meaningful. You choose."

Brian leaned back against the wall, and let the situation sink in. Ten long, uncomfortable seconds passed before Kelly spoke up.

Looking at the board where Brian had written his theory, she explained. "Well, I have to admit that this kind of makes sense."

She paused, hoping someone would break in. They didn't, so she went on. "I mean, we all know that the people in our stores are unhappy. At least the ones who haven't quit are.

And even though the managers come in here and talk a good game to us, I get the feeling that when they go back to their regions, they're as frustrated," she corrected herself, "or maybe I should say *miserable,* as their employees are."

Rob nodded. "My GMs are certainly burnt out. I'm just glad that their counterparts at our competitors are miserable too."

"Well, I have to say that my staff isn't doing that bad."

It was Spencer, but his comment came without much conviction.

Suzanne winced. "You don't think so?"

Spencer shook his head. "That's not the impression I get."

The head of HR continued. "Well, according to the data I have, and the things I've been hearing from your people, your group is actually a little lower than average when it comes to turnover and satisfaction."

"Seriously?"

She nodded gingerly at Spencer, who seemed to accept her assessment.

Brian could see the team was opening up, partly out of desperation, but partly because they were beginning to see the merits of the theory. At least that's what Brian told himself so that he could keep going.

"You guys are going to have to trust me. This is going to work. I've done it before."

He opted against telling them that the only time he had really tested the complete theory was at a tacky little Italian restaurant just off the highway in Tahoe.

"Whether this alone makes all the difference for us financially, I don't know. But it will have a meaningful impact one way or the other."

He paused, aware that a few of the executives were still on the other side of the fence. "And we will certainly be looking hard at decisions around products and geography and pricing, but I honestly don't think that is where the big opportunity is. I really don't."

Brian felt that they might be getting closer to coming around, though still slowly, so he went for the close.

"And now is the part where I get to be a hard-ass." He smiled. "After you take a little time to give this some thought, I want everyone here to let me know whether you're in or you're out. Because I can't let us do this halfway. It will not work if we're not all on board. And I won't take it personally if someone here decides this isn't for them."

Brian still wasn't satisfied with his pitch or his audience's reaction to it, so he exhorted them. "Let me say just one more thing. If you guys do this, your careers will never be the same. You'll go home at the end of the day with a greater sense of satisfaction than you've ever known. That I can guarantee you."

And with that, he turned to erase the board like a professor at the end of a lecture. "I'll be in my office for the rest of the day if anyone wants to come by and talk about this. Because as soon as we know who's in, I can start the process."

Brian was shocked by what happened next.

ON DEMAND

As the group slowly began to disband, Spencer again spoke up. "Wait a second, everybody." The room froze. "Why should we wait until later? Let's do this now."

The silence in the room, and the tone of Spencer's voice, was chilling. To his credit, Spencer continued. "Wow. That sounded a lot more sinister than I intended it to."

A laugh of relief ensued.

"But if this is a good idea—and I'm still not sure it is—then we should figure it out now. That's certainly going to give me a better idea about whether I want to be here."

Lou chimed in. "I'll learn more in here than I will sitting alone in my office."

Brian surveyed the room and decided that the others seemed to agree. "That's fine with me." The executives moved back toward the table.

Brian had mixed feelings about what was happening. On one hand, the next hour would give him a better chance to win the team over than what he'd get from a series of one-on-one meetings. On the other, if he didn't pull it off, the company would probably implode.

"Okay," he said, taking a deep breath, "who wants to go first?"

TRIAL

N o one said anything. Finally, Spencer raised his hand. "I'd like to volunteer," he paused before finishing the sentence, "that Rob go first."

Everyone laughed. Brian was glad for the levity.

"Seriously, though," Spencer explained, "I think we ought to start with one of the regions. I'd be glad to go after Rob."

Heads around the table nodded. Brian got started.

"Okay, Rob. I am your manager, and it is my job to make sure that you feel like I know who you are, that you know how your job matters in someone's life, and that you have an effective way of measuring it. Where should we start?"

"I'll take irrelevance for five hundred, Alex."

Rob's colleagues chuckled at their team clown. Brian hoped the man would be as open-minded as he was funny.

"Why do you want to start there?"

"I don't know. The anonymity thing seems too silly. And I can't imagine that we have any lack of measurement around here. Have you seen the tracking reports that Kelly does?"

They laughed.

Brian wanted to challenge Rob's assessment of anonymity being silly, but decided to go with the flow.

"Okay then, we'll start with irrelevance. Answer this question for me: do you make a meaningful difference in anybody's life? I'm not talking about your family or friends outside work, but here at Desert Mountain."

Just as Rob was about to make a joke, Brian headed him off. "And try to be serious about this, even if it seems silly."

Rob thought hard about it for a few seconds. Finally, he admitted, "Actually, I don't think so. I mean, I can be nice to the people I work with, I suppose. And I can help my GMs hit their targets so they can get their quarterly bonuses. But I'm not sure how meaningful any of that is." He paused. "I'm guessing that's not the answer you were looking for."

Brian smiled. "No, not exactly. But I'll take it because it was honest."

He continued. "Let's take one of your GMs as an example. Who's your youngest or newest GM?"

Rob thought about it. "Probably my guy in Bend, Oregon. Peyton."

"Okay, tell me about Peyton."

Rob frowned, trying to recall what he knew about the man. "He started a few months ago. He's about thirty, was in the army for eight years. Two of his employees quit the week he arrived, and his profitability and revenue numbers are both down."

"Is he frustrated?"

"I certainly hope so. But you wouldn't know it talking to the guy. He always tries to be positive with me. But I'm guessing that he's stressing out quite a bit."

"Does he have a family?"

Rob thought about it. "Yeah, he's married, and I think he has two or three girls and a boy."

Already the looks on the faces in the room were changing, as they considered Petyon's plight. Brian pushed on.

"You think this job matters to Peyton?"

"Yeah, sure. He's got to have some pretty big grocery and diaper bills."

"Beyond that, though. Do you think the level of success he feels, his sense of accomplishment, affects the way he deals with his family, his friends?"

"I don't know. I guess."

"What do you mean, 'you guess'?" It was Suzanne now. "Of course it does!"

Rob relented. "Okay, sure, this job is important to Peyton."

Brian continued his questioning, feeling like a trial lawyer with a witness on the ropes. "How many of his kids are in school?" He didn't wait for an answer. "Do they go to private school? Any medical issues? Do he and his wife own a home? Are they planning on a big family vacation?"

Rob laughed now. "How the hell should I know? I couldn't tell you where my own family is going on vacation this year."

Brian didn't laugh along with him, which made what he was about to say that much more serious. "Here's the thing, Rob. And I think you probably know this deep down inside. You have an opportunity to make a substantial difference in Peyton's life. And in the lives of the other nine GMs you manage. There is probably no other person in the world right now, other than their spouses, who is going to do as much to determine these people's sense of accomplishment and peace of mind."

The room was silent. Riveted.

"And that is the definition of relevant, my friend. And if you don't think that is related to how they do their jobs—" Brian didn't feel the need to finish the sentence.

At first, while Brian was lecturing him, Rob looked like he was being scolded. But now he was nodding his head, in a way that made Brian and everyone else in the room know that he got it.

Now Spencer spoke up. "The next time I see Peyton I think I'm going to have to give him a hug."

The room roared.

Kelly picked up where Brian left off. "So Rob needs to know what's going on with his GMs, and he has to understand that he can impact their lives."

Brian clarified. "He has to *want* to make a difference in their lives."

"Right. What about the measurements?"

"Well, from what I've seen, we have no lack of things that we measure. The question is, are there too many, and is it immediate enough?"

"What do you mean?" the CFO asked, just slightly defensive.

"Well, it's one thing for us to use all the financial and operational data to help us run the company. It would be crazy not to. But Rob can't use that to manage his people every day. There has to be something more regular, more behavioral, that will give Rob a sense of whether they're doing a good job. And he needs them to be able to measure it for themselves."

"What might that be?" Rob asked.

Brian didn't seem to know the answer. "I'm not sure. It depends on how you can influence your GMs most effectively."

Lou asked the best question of the day. "Brian, how are you going to measure yourself as Rob's manager?"

Suddenly everyone was eager to hear the answer. Brian didn't have to think about it long. "I'm going to want to know how much Rob is talking to the GMs. I think he ought to be in regular contact with them, beyond sending them e-mail and reports. I'm certainly going to ask you guys to track your interaction with them," he looked at Frank and Lou.

Brian wasn't finished. "And I'm going to want him to measure how many times he coaches his GMs, either because someone calls him, or because he notices something they need to do better in the stores. The way I see it, if he's doing those things, and taking an interest in what's going on with the GMs, things would have to get better."

Spencer spoke up again. "Don't you think you should be looking at profitability and inventory?"

Brian didn't mind having to answer the question twice; it was critical that his people understand the concept. "Of course. Just not every day. See, management is an everyday thing. Strategy and financial reporting and planning are not."

More than one of the executives in the room wrote that down.

"Okay then, when I roll this out in my organization, what should I have my GMs measuring?" It was Rob now, and he seemed eager to have an answer. "I'm guessing it has something to do with how they're dealing with their employees."

Brian nodded. Lou chimed in.

"I recently came to the conclusion that the best GMs are the ones who spend less time at the register and dealing with customers, and more time giving employees immediate feedback about what they're doing wrong, or right."

"So why aren't they doing that now?" Brian asked.

Frank hit the nail on the head. "Because we're making them fill out reports all day, and we're not teaching them how to manage their people."

That was exactly the endorsement Brian was looking for.

Though part of Brian wanted to keep pushing, he could see that his staff was a bit overwhelmed, and that there wasn't much time left until some of the team would have to leave for another meeting.

"Okay, let's talk about this again next week. In the meantime, Rob, I'd appreciate it if you could stick around for a few minutes, we can talk about how to go about testing this in one of your stores."

After everyone had gone, the two of them spent the next hour coming up with a plan. Brian was surprised at the aggressiveness of Rob's ideas, and how much the class clown seemed to have bought into his program.

ONE FELL SWOOP

The plan called for Brian, Rob, and one of his GMs to meet with all of a store's employees during off-hours for a comprehensive discussion of how they were going to transform the way people were managed, and how they would treat customers.

Brian liked the idea from the beginning, and his enthusiasm only grew after a little personal research at the local store.

Actually, Brian didn't conduct the reconnaissance himself; he asked Leslie to do it for him. She agreed without hesitation. "Besides, I need new sneakers and snow boots anyway." Her experience at the store proved an interesting one.

First, it wound up taking more than twenty minutes for someone to offer to help her. Second, when she asked for advice about a product, not only was the employee unable to provide an answer, he made no attempt to find one. Finally, though the shoes Leslie bought were on sale, the cashier rang them up at regular price, and when Leslie caught the error, the cashier seemed annoyed that she'd have to redo the transaction.

Based on that information, it wasn't difficult for Brian to convince Rob to use the Tahoe store for their pilot program—what Rob called "the intervention." The store was a good choice not only because it had serious issues with employee retention and customer service but because its proximity to the Bailey household would make it easier for the CEO to monitor its progress.

On Monday evening, the night before the event, Brian and Rob met with the Tahoe GM, Eric, to explain what they were trying to accomplish and prep him as well as they could for what was about to happen to his business. That he wasn't completely comfortable with the idea didn't concern Brian, who was convinced that making people a little uncomfortable was exactly what the company needed.

By the next morning at eight o'clock, a full two hours before the store would open for business, all fifteen staff members were at work. Eric had created a space for the meeting by taking down a few of the display tents in the camping section and dragging over all of the little benches from the shoe department.

Rob, whom Brian was liking more and more with every day they spent together, kicked off the session with the best introduction Brian had ever heard.

"Thanks for coming in today, everyone. The reason we're here is because our company is in trouble. I'm sure that's not a surprise to you. Our revenue is slowly shrinking. Our competitors are taking away our business, and by that, I mean customers. And some of our best people have left over the past year."

He paused to let the reality sink in. "Now, that doesn't mean that every store is doing poorly. Some are doing better than others." He paused again, so that his next point would be particularly clear. "This is not one of those stores."

Most of the employees, including Eric, who was seated behind Rob, seemed a little less comfortable now. Rob continued.

"And you know whose fault that is?" Rob paused yet again, but didn't wait for an answer. "It's partly yours." He motioned to his audience. "The service our employees have been giving customers has been poor."

After letting it sink in, he went on. "But more of the blame falls on Eric." He turned to the slightly shocked GM. "After all, he's responsible for this store." Eric tried unsuccessfully to look impassive about the comment, as though he had expected his boss to make the statement.

"But even more than Eric, I'm to blame. After all, I'm responsible for the Nevada stores."

And then he turned to Brian. "And this guy here. He's our new CEO. Six months from now, if things aren't any better, then it will be his fault. After all, he runs the company."

After one last pause, Rob finished his sermon. "And so, I don't see why we wouldn't want to listen to what he has to say, and do what he wants us to do. Because when you look at our situation, we don't really have anything to lose. Hell, we're already losing."

And with that, he turned to his new boss. "Brian?"

The mood in the room was now unsurprisingly melancholy.

"Okay, I want to ask everyone a question. But don't answer right away. Just think about it for a second." He paused. "Do you think you have a good job?"

Brian let the question sit there. "This job at Desert Mountain, do you think it qualifies as a good job?"

After letting them think about it for a moment, he tried to provoke an answer. "Anyone want to start?"

For the next few minutes, members of the staff shared their answers, ranging from "I don't know" to "maybe" to "yes,

I think so." A woman in her mid-twenties offered the most honest answer.

"I hope I'm not stepping out of line here," she looked at Eric, "but I don't think this is a particularly good job."

Brian encouraged her. "No, that's not at all out of line. I want you to be honest. Tell me what you consider to be a good job. Who do you know that has a good job?"

She thought about it. "I think a good job is one where you don't have to work much and you get paid a lot of money." The other staff members chuckled.

Brian pushed on. "Okay, who do you know that has a job like that?"

"You mean, who do I know personally?"

"Not necessarily. I mean, what kind of job would that be? Who has a job like that?"

"I don't know." Then something occurred to her. "Maybe a model."

Brian nodded as though he agreed. "Okay, a fashion model. Some of the famous ones get paid quite a bit and don't seem to have to work too hard. That makes sense."

The young woman was pleased that the CEO seemed to have confirmed her answer.

"Do you think that most models like their jobs?"

No one answered, so Brian went on. "I mean, it seems to me that a lot of them have eating disorders and relationship issues and drug problems. I don't know about you, but I've never really looked at models and thought, 'Now, there's a group of people who seem really happy.'"

The staff members demonstrated their agreement with Brian's assessment by laughing and nodding their heads.

Another employee raised his hand. "I think being a professional athlete sounds pretty good."

Brian was glad to have more participation. "And why is that?"

"Well, they get paid a lot for doing something fun in front of millions of people."

Brian nodded, but with a frown on his face. "Okay, I guess that some athletes do get paid a lot for having fun. But not too many of them make it to that level. And it seems to me that even many of those that do aren't all that happy. I mean, a lot of them get in trouble for beating their wives or doing drugs, or they end up blowing all their money."

Now Eric spoke up. "Most of you already know that I played professional baseball. For the Rangers. I made it to Double-A, which is pretty close to the majors. If you can believe it, I didn't make as much money then as I do now, and I wasn't having much fun. The minor leagues are a grind until you get to the top."

The audience seemed both interested and surprised by what Eric said.

Someone in the back shouted a question. "What about being a CEO? That sounds like a sweet deal to me."

More laughter among the employees.

Brian smiled. "I'm not going to lie to you. I do like being a CEO. I really do. But many of the CEOs I know aren't all that happy. In fact, I'd say that more of them are unsatisfied in their jobs than are happy. And that's the truth."

People seemed surprised, if not a little wary, at the comment from their CEO.

Brian continued, "What do you think makes a job a good one? Beyond money, what is it that makes someone like their work?"

Having warmed up a little, more of the employees offered their opinions, ranging from a comfortable environment to a fair boss to the freedom to make their own decisions. One guy gave the most interesting answer when he said, "I just want to win." Brian took it all in.

"All right. I'm going to stop asking questions now, and tell you what I believe, and what we're going to do. And what I'm about to say may not be what everyone wants to hear, and that's okay, because no one has to work here. I won't hate you if you decide you don't want to be part of our new reality, but I think most of you are going to like it."

He paused to let a little suspense build. "First, I think people deserve to like their jobs, and that it's up to managers to make that possible. From now on, Eric's job is going to be about working hard to help you like your work. Just like Rob is going to do for him, and I'm going to do for Rob."

The looks on the employees' faces mixed skepticism and hope.

"Second, I think a company deserves to have its employees care about the business and do their best to make it successful. From now on, people are going to be held accountable for doing what's right for Desert Mountain and our customers."

He smiled. "It is my sincere hope that in the next few weeks and months, everyone who wants to be here will like coming to work more than they do now, that customers will like shopping here more than they do now, and that our CFO, Kelly, will take longer to count our money than she does now."

Employees laughed politely.

"And here's how it's going to work."

Brian then delivered his twenty-minute talk on the dangers of immeasurement and irrelevance. He decided that anonymity was something only Eric needed to hear, and that telling employees about it would only make it seem contrived.

The staff broke out into two groups, led by Brian and Rob, and worked to identify one another's key measurements as well as the people whose lives they impacted. After just over an hour, both Rob and Eric began to feel that the employees seemed to have a slightly new level of energy.

With just fifteen minutes until the doors would open, Brian thanked Eric and his staff for their time and assured them that he would be coming back from time to time to see how they were doing. And even to buy running shoes when his knee healed.

As he left the store with Rob, Brian felt more confident than ever about his theory, and the impact it could have on Desert Mountain Sports.

ROLLOUT

For the next two months, Brian and his regional VPs went to every last one of the company's twenty-four stores, conducting two-hour interventions much like the one in Tahoe. But changing the culture of a sizable organization takes time, and seeing the financial benefits takes even longer.

Some of the stores started off better than others, and some needed a lot of attention from executives at headquarters. A few managers opted out of the experiment and left DMS, but most got on board.

During the rest of the summer, Brian spent much of his time coaching his team on how to go about coaching their people, especially the GMs. He continued traveling to reinforce his program, but never on Mondays or Fridays, as he had promised Leslie.

When he wasn't ridding the company of immeasurement, irrelevance, and anonymity, he seemed to be spending much of his time with investment banks and board members, assuring them that selling the company too soon would be a mistake, and that eventually the company's performance would improve enough to warrant a much higher selling price.

Finally, as his six-month anniversary at Desert Mountain approached, Brian received the news he had been hoping for. It was Kelly, his CFO, who delivered it during one of the team's weekly meetings.

"Ladies and gentlemen, we have officially started growing again." The team burst out into spontaneous applause.

MOMENTUM

Over the course of the next three months, improvement at DMS accelerated. Two stores that had been slated for closure were now being kept open, and a new superstore in Oregon was being discussed at staff meetings.

Of course, the good news meant that the board and investment bankers would be renewing their interest in selling the company. As he prepared for his third quarterly board meeting since taking over as CEO, Brian had mixed feelings.

As usual, he asked his wife to help him sort it out.

"The board thinks I'm a hero, because they're going to get 20 or 25 percent more from a buyer now."

"Isn't that what they hired you to do?" she asked.

"Yeah, but I think there is more improvement to be made, and that selling out right now would be a mistake. I have a few other ideas."

Leslie frowned now, but in a playful way. "I was afraid you'd say that."

That evening at the board meeting, Rick Simpson presented the likely suitors who would be interested in buying DMS at a higher price than before. As he concluded, he turned to Brian and asked for his opinion on which of them he would prefer.

"I'd have to say that Northwest Athletics is my first choice."

Almost all of the board members were surprised by the answer. So was Rick.

"But they're in a weaker market position than any of the others, and would probably make a lower bid. I don't think selling to them would make sense, Brian."

"Oh, I agree with you completely," Brian informed his confused audience. "I wasn't thinking about them buying us. I'm thinking we should buy them."

The reaction of the board members ranged from shock to curiosity. Rick just smiled. In the end, a decision was made to keep operating Desert Mountain independently for a few months, and then reassess at the beginning of winter.

By the time December arrived, discussion during the board meetings shifted from how to sell the company to how to make it grow. With every month, the finances looked a little stronger, and the competitive landscape began to change. By the new year, Brian and his reenergized executive team were making serious plans to acquire Northwest Athletics as well as a smaller competitor in California, confident they could do for those struggling companies what they had done for DMS.

And then it all came to a screeching halt.

SUCKER PUNCH

At the first board meeting of the new year, as Brian was getting ready to present his plan for acquiring the two companies he and his staff had identified, the chairman of the board announced that he had agreed to sell Desert Mountain to one of the nation's largest retailers for 60 percent more than what they had been expecting less than a year earlier.

Brian couldn't believe it.

None of the other board members, with the exception of Rick Simpson, seemed at all aware of the shock that Brian was feeling. The chairman even went so far as to congratulate his CEO for what he had done to make the deal possible.

After the meeting was over, Rick and Brian went for a beer.

"I tried to talk them out of it, Brian, but it was hard. I mean, the whole reason I'm on the board was to help them do this deal. As much as I would have liked to see them change course, it just wasn't something they wanted to do. They own the company, and they wanted out."

Though Brian wasn't about to blame Rick, he couldn't help but argue the point. "But we could have found investors and done a buy-out or something. Couldn't we?"

Rick nodded. "Yes, and you could have run the company for the next five years and then sold it to some other bigger company for even more money. And you didn't want to do that, did you?"

Brian thought about it. "No, not if I wanted to stay married. But it just seems like such a shame."

"Why?"

Brian was just a bit incredulous now. "Because there are people out there in our stores who have worked hard to turn this thing around, and who actually like their jobs for a change. I hate to see that disappear."

"Who's to say that it will disappear?"

"Come on, Rick. You know what's going to happen. You think that a seventeen-billion-dollar company is going to let them run the stores the way we've been doing it?"

He shook his head. "Probably not. But that's not going to happen for a year or two. And besides, that's not the point, is it?"

"What do you mean?"

"I mean, those people are going to keep working and managing and they'll take those ideas of yours to the next place they go. Isn't that the point?"

Brian took a drink of his beer. "I guess so. I don't know."

DÉJÀ VU

After taking a few weeks to wrap up his stint at DMS, Brian found himself in limbo yet again. He and Leslie faced another decision about the next phase of their retirement, albeit with a slightly different perspective now.

Though they joked about it, there was no way that Brian was going to go back to work at Gene and Joe's again. But he wasn't ready to retire again either. Leslie could see that now. Ideally, Brian wanted to find another adventure, one with equal parts flexibility and challenge.

For a few months, Brian was content to just ski with Leslie, pop in on his friends at the pizza place down the street, and read the *Wall Street Journal* from time to time without guilt.

And then another call came from Rick Simpson.

ENCORE

A company in London, an upscale hotel chain, needed consulting help with employee satisfaction issues that were having a pronounced impact on customers.

"If you can help them cut turnover even a little," Rick explained, "it could transform their financial position drastically. And it would give you a chance to work your magic on an even larger scale," he added playfully. "And I'll have you out of there in six months, seven tops."

Brian and Leslie didn't have to talk about it for long. They had always wanted to live abroad, but could never break away from their children's baseball and basketball and soccer and ballet schedules.

"We would be crazy not to do this!" Leslie declared.

Six weeks later the Baileys were settled into their apartment in Kensington Gardens, in the center of London. For the rest of the year they enjoyed Brian's work more than ever, doing market research in five-star hotels throughout the United Kingdom and across the Continent, with great success.

Brian was thrilled to confirm that his ideas about ending misery at work applied in yet another industry, and outside the boundaries of the United States. But he was even happier about a package he received from the United States one evening. The postmark was from South Lake Tahoe, and the return address was the restaurant. Standing in the kitchen while Leslie made dinner, he opened the box and discovered what appeared to be two Gene and Joe's T-shirts inside. Pulling them out and unfolding them, Brian found himself speechless as he realized what he was looking at.

Beneath a picture of two smiling faces were the words "Migo and Joe's: Pizza and Pasta. Here, There, Everywhere."

The Model

THE MISERABLE JOB

Amiserable job is not the same as a bad one.

As with beauty, the definition of a bad job lies in the eye of the beholder. Some people consider a job bad because it is physically demanding or exhausting, involving long hours in the hot sun. Others see it as one that doesn't pay well. Still others call a job bad because it requires a long commute or a great deal of time sitting behind a desk. It really depends on who you are and what you value and enjoy.

However, everyone knows what a miserable job is.

It's the one you dread going to and can't wait to leave. It's the one that saps your energy even when you're not busy. It's the one that makes you go home at the end of the day with less enthusiasm and more cynicism than you had when you left in the morning.

Miserable jobs are found everywhere—consulting firms, television stations, banks, schools, churches, software companies, professional football teams, amusement parks. And they exist at all levels, from the executive suite to the reception desk to the mail room.

It's important to understand that being miserable has nothing to do with the actual work a job involves. A professional basketball player can be miserable in his job while the janitor cleaning the locker room behind him finds fulfillment in his work. A marketing executive can be miserable making a quarter of a million dollars a year while the waitress who serves her lunch derives meaning and satisfaction from her job.

That's the thing about misery at work. It makes little sense and knows no bounds. No one is immune.

THE COST OF MISERY

I would be impossible to accurately measure the amount of misery in the workforce, but my experience tells me this: more people out there are miserable in their jobs than fulfilled by them. And the cost of this, in both economic and human terms, is staggering.

Economically, productivity suffers greatly when employees are unfulfilled. The effects on a company's bottom line or a nation's economy are undeniable. But it's the social cost of misery at work that seems particularly overwhelming, because it has such a broad ripple effect.

A miserable employee goes home at the end of the day frustrated, cynical, and weary and spreads that frustration, cynicism, and weariness to others—spouses, children, friends, strangers on the bus. Even the most emotionally mature, self-aware people cannot help but let work misery leak into the rest of their lives.

What is the result of this leakage? In some cases it is extra family stress and tension, and the inability to appreciate the blessings in life. As amorphous as that may seem, over time it impacts people's emotional and psychological health in profound and potentially irreversible ways. In some situations, though, job misery leads to even more immediate and tangible problems, like drug and alcohol abuse, or violence.

It's difficult to accurately estimate the magnitude of the problems caused by miserable jobs. And while no job will ever be perfect, and no society will be without its economic and social problems related to work, if there were a meaningful way to reduce job misery, without cost, wouldn't that be worth doing?

I think so too. The first step lies in understanding the root causes of a miserable job.

THE THREE SIGNS

Three underlying factors will make a job miserable, and they can apply to virtually all jobs regardless of the nature of the work being done. The three signs are at first glance obvious and seemingly easy to resolve. And yet they remain largely unaddressed in most organizations.

ANONYMITY

People cannot be fulfilled in their work if they are not known. All human beings need to be understood and appreciated for their unique qualities by someone in a position of authority. As much as this may sound like an aphorism from *Mr. Rogers' Neighborhood,* it is undeniably true. People who see themselves as invisible, generic, or anonymous cannot love their jobs, no matter what they are doing.

IRRELEVANCE

Everyone needs to know that their job matters, to someone. Anyone. Without seeing a connection between the work and the satisfaction of another person or group of people, an employee simply will not find lasting fulfillment. Even the most cynical employees need to know that their work matters to someone, even if it's just the boss.

IMMEASUREMENT

Employees need to be able to gauge their progress and level of contribution for themselves. They cannot be fulfilled in their work if their success depends on the opinions or whims of another person, no matter how benevolent that person may be. Without a tangible means for assessing success or failure, motivation eventually deteriorates as people see themselves as unable to control their own fate.

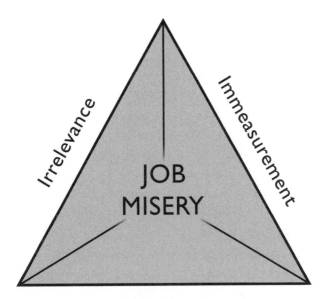

Simple? Absolutely.

Obvious? Perhaps.

But if so, then why in the world do so many managers—dare I say, most managers—fail to provide their people with these basics of a meaningful job?

Maybe because it is too obvious. Well-educated people often have a hard time getting their hands around simple solutions. Or perhaps the eighteenth-century author Samuel Johnson is right, and they just need to be reminded a lot. Or maybe they're just not sure about how to get started.

Whatever the case, the following sections provide a deeper understanding of the three signs of a miserable job, the benefits of addressing them, and what is needed to make any job more fulfilling.

THE BENEFITS
AND OBSTACLES
OF MANAGING FOR
JOB FULFILLMENT

BENEFITS

The benefits to an organization that can build a culture of job fulfillment—and the issues that prevent us from realizing those benefits—are worth exploring before outlining a job fulfillment program: increased productivity, greater retention and lower costs, and cultural differentiation.

Increased Productivity

Employees who find fulfillment in their jobs are going to work with more enthusiasm, passion, and attention to quality than their counterparts who do not, mostly because they develop a sense of ownership and pride in what they are doing. That means they'll arrive earlier, stay later, pitch in outside their areas of responsibility, and look for ways to improve their performance, all without being asked.

Greater Retention and Lower Costs

Simply stated, employees hang onto fulfilling jobs as long as they can, mostly because they know that their chances of finding another are relatively slim. What is more, fulfilled employees tend to attract other good employees to an organization, either by actively recruiting them or merely by telling friends about their enthusiasm for their work. The result of all this for an organization is significantly lower costs related to recruiting, hiring, retraining, and termination.

Sustainable Cultural Differentiation

The opportunity for differentiation from competitors by building a culture of job fulfillment cannot be overstated. In a world of ubiquitous technology and rapid dissemination of information, it is harder and harder to establish sustainable competitive advantage through strategic and tactical decision making. Cultural differentiation, however, is more valuable than it's ever been, because it requires courage and discipline more than creativity or intelligence.

Along these lines, managers who work to reduce the three signs in their organizations discover an unexpected side effect. Employees themselves begin to take a greater interest in their colleagues, help them find meaning and relevance in their work, and find better ways to gauge their own success, and they do all of this without specific direction from their bosses. In essence, they take some responsibility for keeping the three signs of a miserable job at bay. Ironically, this gives them yet a greater sense of meaning while creating a sustainable cultural advantage that competitors will envy but find difficult to duplicate.

OBSTACLES

So what are the obstacles that prevent so many employees and managers, and the companies they work for, from tapping into this opportunity?

Employee Obstacles

Employees often fail to find fulfillment in their work because they place too much emphasis on maximizing compensation or choosing the right career. Are these irrelevant? Of course not. Even if you love what you do, if you can't feed your family or earn a livable wage, you have a problem on your hands. And if you're meant to be a carpenter and you find yourself sitting behind a desk doing accounting, then your ceiling on job fulfillment is going to be low.

However, even people who are relatively well paid for doing what they love (such as professional athletes, executives, and actors) are often miserable if they feel anonymous, their job is irrelevant, or their work is not objectively measurable. Consider that the world is full of advice on how to make more money and how to choose the right career, and yet people remain miserable. And even people who aren't doing their dream job and making a ton of money in the process will usually find satisfaction if their managers are reducing anonymity, irrelevance, and immeasurement in their jobs.

Organizational Obstacles

When it comes to managers and the companies where they work, the obstacles to eliminating misery are different. Too often, they are slow to recognize that they have an employee satisfaction issue, and then when they finally do, their attempts to address it focus on the wrong issues.

Many companies only come to terms with the fact that they have a job fulfillment problem when employees start to leave. Unfortunately, during exit interviews, people tend to report that they are leaving because their next employer is going to pay them more money. This provokes human resources professionals—and the executives who listen to them—to raise salaries and other forms of compensation in spite of the fact that the last time they did so resulted in no lasting or sustainable improvements in employee retention, satisfaction, or productivity.

The problem, of course, is that departing employees rarely tell the whole story. By the time people decide to leave an organization, they have little incentive to tell their soon-to-be-former employer the truth—that they are leaving because their supervisor didn't really manage them, and without a good manager, their jobs eventually became miserable. What companies should be doing is asking a different question, and far sooner than an exit interview: *What is making you even consider leaving in the first place?*

Even in those instances when executives are able to discern that poor management is the real source of employee dissatisfaction, their response, though well-intentioned, is rarely effective. That response usually takes the form of more management training, which often includes mandatory classes on setting goals, writing performance evaluations, and giving feedback. And while those are certainly topics worthy of attention, the impact of these kinds of classes is almost never immediate, and is all too often negligible.

That's partly because goals cannot be set, reviews cannot be written, and even feedback cannot easily be given immediately after a training class ends. Organizations have cycles and schedules and calendars that indicate when these things need to be done. And by the time those dates roll around, managers who attended the classes have either forgotten about the skills they learned or been distracted by some other overriding priority from the top. Or most likely, both.

What managers need is something that is both less mechanical and more emotionally, fundamentally, and immediately tied to the job satisfaction of employees. And that is where the elimination of anonymity, irrelevance, and immeasurement comes into play.

The Emotional Obstacle

Even when managers understand and appreciate the importance of addressing the three signs, they very often struggle to do so because of a natural behavioral shortcoming of their own. This is a critical point to understand

In order to be the kind of leader who demonstrates genuine interest in employees and who can help people discover the relevance of their work, a person must have a level of personal confidence and emotional vulnerability. Without it, managers will often feel uncomfortable, even embarrassed, about having such simple, behavioral conversations with their employees. They'll mistakenly feel like kindergarten teachers or little league coaches delivering a simplistic pep talk, even though their employees—at all levels—are yearning for just such a conversation.

EXPLORING AND ADDRESSING THE CAUSES OF JOB MISERY

ANONYMITY

It is immensely more difficult to decide to leave an organization or a team (or a family for that matter) when you feel that others on the team know and understand you as an individual. And the person who can have the greatest influence by taking a personal interest in anyone on the job is the manager. Yes, even more than a CEO or an executive three levels higher in the food chain, a direct supervisor needs to take a genuine, personal interest in an employee in order to increase that employee's satisfaction and fulfillment.

What exactly does it mean to take a personal interest in someone? I've heard management training people advise supervisors to listen to the music that their employees listen to and watch the television shows that they watch. Though I suppose that could be helpful in some situations, it doesn't seem to be a terribly useful first step.

First, it could come across as disingenuous and silly when a fifty-year-old plant manager starts talking about listening to hip hop and watching *MTV Cribs* (which, for the record, I've never watched). Employees can smell a false attempt at "employee bonding" from a mile away. The other problem with cultural mirroring (if there is such a thing) is that it is general and stereotypical in nature and often reinforces to employees that they are seen as somewhat generic.

A better way to remove any sense of anonymity or invisibility from employees' situation at work is simply to *get to know them*. Take time to sit down with each of them and ask them what's going on in their lives. Some managers reflexively avoid this because they've been taught that it is illegal to ask that kind of question during job interviews. Somehow they forget that what may be illegal when selecting a candidate is actually a basic form of human kindness once someone has been hired.

But it can't be fake. When I say that a manager needs to take an interest in an employee, I'm talking about taking *a genuine interest*. To manage another human being effectively requires some degree of empathy and curiosity about why that person gets out of bed in the morning, what is on their mind, and how you can contribute to them becoming a better person.

And taking a personal interest in an employee is not a one-time thing either, something to be checked off on a list of to-dos. It needs to be reinforced and demonstrated again and again. It's one thing to know that an employee's daughter likes dancing. It's quite another to ask how Friday's dance recital went. And it's fine to know that a subordinate lives with his parents. It's another thing entirely to know their names and ask about them when they're sick.

Okay, if any of this sounds hokey, consider whether you have appreciated it when your manager took an interest, a real one, in you and your life. And if you're rolling your eyes at this point, wondering what any of this has to do with software development or factory line assembly or accounting, put up with me as I remind you that no one gets out of bed in the morning to program software or assemble furniture or do whatever it is that accountants do. They get out of bed to live their lives, and their work tasks are only a part of their lives. People want to be managed as people, not as mere workers.

If you're still not convinced that this makes sense or that it applies to you, this would be a good time to consider resigning your position as a manager and finding a role as an individual contributor. But if you're on board, there are two more fundamental dragons that need to be slain.

IRRELEVANCE

People wonder why so many athletes, rock stars, and actors live such erratic, unsatisfied lives. It's easy to point to drugs and alcohol and materialism as the culprits, but I think those are mere symptoms of the root cause: a subtle fear of irrelevance.

I mention this because it's hard to fathom how someone who earns more money than most people can count by doing something they love, and who gets constant attention and adulation from admiring fans, can be unhappy. And how a nurse in a home for the elderly, or a receptionist at a church, or a high-school volleyball coach can be happy in spite of the fact they make a fraction of what a rock star or athlete makes. I think the answer has everything to do with being needed. Having an impact on the lives of others.

Human beings need to be needed, and they need to be reminded of this pretty much every day. They need to know that they are helping others, not merely serving themselves.

When people lose sight of their impact on other people's lives, or worse yet, when they come to the realization that they have no impact at all, they begin to die emotionally. The fact is, God didn't create people to serve themselves. Everyone ultimately wants and needs to help others, and when they cannot, misery ensues.

Some will say that rock stars and athletes and actors do indeed have an impact on other people's lives, and I would agree that they certainly can. However, they often lose sight of that impact or fail to take advantage of their opportunity to do so. They see their jobs as a series of self-involved activities with no clear connection to the daily lives of others.

All employees, whether they are rock stars, software engineers, or teachers, must answer two questions in order to establish relevance in their jobs. And it is the manager's responsibility to help them do this.

Who?

The first question people have to answer is, Who am I helping? The most obvious place to start looking is among customers. For flight attendants, fast-food cashiers, teachers, priests, doctors, waiters, and salespeople, this is an easy choice. But for many employees outside the service businesses, from the CEO to the accounting clerk to the head of IT, interaction with customers is a relatively rare occurrence.

For those people, the answer is often "internal customers," other employees or departments within the organization. Some may hear this and say "everyone within our company should be serving customers," and I would agree. But that doesn't mean that customers are the primary people whose lives everyone can count on affecting on a daily basis, or that people are going to derive satisfaction from having an impact on someone they rarely if ever encounter.

For a CEO, the answer to the question of "whose life do you impact" will certainly include "the executive team." For the accountants, it will probably be the head of finance, or whatever department within the company they support. And for many—brace yourself—the answer will often be their boss.

That's right. Seemingly contrary to everything we've learned having to do with servant leadership (a concept I love, by the way), sometimes managers must help their employees understand that their work has a meaningful impact on them. This is a hard concept to swallow because it conjures up images of self-serving supervisors sending their employees on personal errands and keeping them at their beck and call. And so managers often downplay the very real impact that the work their employees do has on their own satisfaction and career development.

And this is its own tragedy because, unless they already believe that their manager is a cretin, employees get a great deal of satisfaction and energy when their supervisor thanks them for what they've done and explains to them what a difference they've made for them personally.

233

Think about this one again. It is our fear of coming across as self-serving that prevents us from giving our employees the satisfaction of knowing that they've helped us. Ironically, the result is that they feel that we are taking them for granted.

Managers would be much better off being frank with employees. "The report you put together for my presentation to the executive team was terrific. They were all impressed, and wanted me to tell you that you did a nice job. And I want to tell you that you've made me, and the entire department, stand out in the eyes of the CEO. Thanks." That's a far cry from "you made me look like a champ today, and I won't forget the little people like you when I become rich and famous." And it's certainly better than the generic, "you did a great job."

When managers pretend that they don't appreciate the impact of their people's work on their own career and job satisfaction—even when they do it out of humility!—they deprive people of the feeling that they've made a difference.

How?

The next question that managers need to help employees answer is "how am I helping?" And the answer to this question is not always obvious.

When a room service attendant at the Embassy Suites next to the airport brings breakfast to a guest, he's not just delivering food. He's helping a weary traveler feel a little better about having to be on the road, which can have a significant impact on their outlook on life that day.

And when a clerk in the billing department at a doctor's office helps a patient find a receipt for an appointment six months earlier, she's not merely providing them with information. She's giving them peace of mind so that they can be a little less stressed about managing their family's health care, something that causes its own health problems.

Some managers will wince at all this. They'll say, "Come on, the room service guy is carrying breakfast and the billing clerk is doing paperwork." Which leads us to the central point here. If managers cannot see beyond what their employees are doing and help them understand who they are helping and how they are making a difference, then those jobs are bound to be miserable.

Keep in mind that employees at Southwest Airlines are doing largely the same job as employees at any other large airline, and yet there are far fewer miserable jobs at Southwest. And high school kids at In-N-Out Burger and Chick-fil-A are doing largely the same job that kids at any other fast-food restaurant are doing, and yet there are a lot fewer miserable jobs at In-N-Out and Chick-fil-A.

The difference is not the job itself. It is the management. And one of the most important things that managers must do is help employees see why their work matters to someone. Even if this sounds touchy-feely to some, it is a fundamental part of human nature.

IMMEASUREMENT

First, let me say that immeasurement isn't a word you'll find in the dictionary. I've used it to describe this, the third sign of a miserable job, because there was no real synonym for it. Immeasurement essentially is an employee's lack of a clear means of assessing his or her progress or success on the job. This creates ambiguity and a feeling of dependence on a manager to subjectively judge the employee's daily or weekly or monthly achievement.

The problem is, great employees don't want their success to depend on the subjective views or opinions of another human being. That's because this often forces them to engage in politics and posturing, which is distasteful for a variety of reasons, not the least of which is the loss of control over one's destiny. Employees who can measure their own progress or contribution are going to develop a greater sense of personal responsibility and satisfaction than those who cannot.

The key to establishing effective measures for a job lies in identifying those areas that an employee can directly influence, and then ensuring that the specific measurements are connected to the person or people they are meant to serve. This point is worth repeating. Failing to link measurement to relevance is illogical and creates confusion among employees, who are left wondering why they aren't measuring the most important parts of their jobs.

Too often, an executive will try to rally employees by giving them some macro objective (for example, hitting a corporate revenue number, cutting company expenses, or driving up the stock price).

The problem here is that most employees have no direct impact on these things, certainly not on a daily basis. When they realize that there is no clear, observable link between their daily job responsibilities and the metric they are going to be measured against, they lose interest and feel unable to control their own destiny. And while many managers will then be tempted to accuse them of being lazy or ignoring the well-being of the company, those managers are failing to understand that what their employees are looking for is a measure that is more closely tied to their actual jobs.

That's why so many salespeople enjoy their jobs. They don't depend on others to tell them whether they've succeeded or failed. At the end of the day—or better yet, the quarter—a salesperson knows the score and feels responsible for it.

Sports is another arena where measurables are clear (though anonymity and irrelevance are often problems). Imagine a basketball game where no score is kept, but where a winner is chosen based on the subjective criteria of judges. Sound miserable?

Or consider a pitcher coming off the mound with no statistical evidence of his own performance, but dependent on the gut feel of his coach. Unfortunately, that is all too common in the way many employees are managed and assessed.

Unlike sports, business measurements need not be completely quantitative to be effective. In many cases, trying to overquantify measurables by assigning strictly numerical metrics makes them irrelevant because the metric is artificial. The most effective and appropriate measurements are often behavioral in nature and might simply call for an informal survey of customers, or even merely an observation of behavior that indicates satisfaction.

Ironically, a measurable need not be tied to compensation to be effective. In fact, psychological research would indicate that connecting it to pay can sometimes actually decrease incentive. Whether or not that is true in a given situation, the point is that people want measurables so that they can get an intrinsic sense of accomplishment. Great athletes don't get excited about scoring goals or running for touchdowns because they know it will impact their contracts—though they're certainly not going to turn the money down. They do it because they love to compete.

Cynics may disagree with this. They might point to salespeople and accuse them of being coin-operated, motivated primarily by money. In reality, most great salespeople are motivated primarily by winning, by achieving a goal. Yes, that goal is tied to compensation, but the money itself is gravy. That's why so many salespeople get involved in other competitive pursuits, athletic or otherwise. They love to compete and to win, whether the reward is financial or not.

CASE STUDIES

Okay, enough theory. It's time to see what the three signs might look like when applied.

What follows are a number of examples of how managers in various industries and at all levels might go about making an employee's job more fulfilling. Some of the illustrations are relatively straightforward and easy to figure out, while others are decidedly unique and require more creativity on the part of a manager. Whatever the case, they are all immensely doable for leaders who have the courage and boldness to be different for the sake of their employees.

EXAMPLE I: THE VICE PRESIDENT OF MARKETING

Nancy is the head of marketing at a medium-sized software company. She reports to the CEO and oversees everything from branding and advertising to product marketing and the design of the company's Web site. Why might she be miserable?

Anonymity

There is a decent chance that anonymity is a factor. As is often the case among senior executives, the CEO she reports to has little time or inclination to take a personal interest in the lives of his subordinates, people he sees as needing little supervision and support. He has to remember that senior executives like Nancy have just as much need as line employees do for their manager to know and understand them as people, even if they will rarely come right out and say it. That doesn't mean the CEO should patronize Nancy with questions about her inner child. But it does require him to develop a genuine concern for what is going on in Nancy's life and career. As soft as that may sound, it matters to Nancy, and it will improve her performance.

Irrelevance

Many executives like Nancy eventually lose a sense of meaning in their work. Now that she is earning a comfortable living and has achieved a high degree of success in her career, she often wonders what the larger purpose of her work should be. As her manager, the CEO needs to help her connect personally to the company's mission and its impact on customers, or to give her a sense of how she can influence the lives of her staff and make them more successful and fulfilled in their careers—or both. He also needs to help her understand how she might be making his life or career better by doing a good job.

Immeasurement

This is an area where Nancy may not be lacking too much overall, as most executives have plenty of data and often rely on quantitative analysis to do their jobs. However, it is entirely possible that many of her measurements are disconnected from the meaningful purpose of her job. The CEO should have her monitor the progress she is making with her people, in addition, of course, to measuring the overall impact of her programs.

By the way, Nancy has an administrative assistant named Jenny. . . .

EXAMPLE 2: THE ADMINISTRATIVE ASSISTANT

Jenny's responsibilities include scheduling, communication, and general assistance to her boss. She has virtually no interaction with the company's customers, and she spends much of her energy protecting Nancy from people who are constantly demanding her time. Jenny feels underappreciated at times and beaten down by having to be the gatekeeper who says no to so many people every day.

Anonymity

In this case, anonymity is not the likely problem for Jenny, though it could be an issue. To eliminate this, Jenny's manager should take an interest in her as a person, as well as any aspirations she might have. Nancy can make up for Jenny's limited career path options by giving her personal development opportunities, and by nurturing—yes, nurturing—the special one-on-one relationship that is unique for each executive-and-assistant pairing.

Irrelevance

Nancy needs to take the time to remind Jenny how much her work impacts her own ability to serve the company as an executive. She needs to help Jenny realize the influence she has on her career, and how the decisions she makes as an assistant affect her personally as well. Of course, to avoid making Jenny feel like her success is dependent on the mood of the marketing VP, she will need to help her establish a way to measure her effectiveness as objectively as possible.

Immeasurement

The best way to go about establishing a relevant measurable is to think about assessing the various ways that Jenny impacts her boss's work life, which in turn helps the company. That might include a weekly review of how much time is set aside for strategic planning and creative thinking, the responsiveness of communication with key constituents within the company, and the avoidance of unnecessary meetings and interruptions.

By the way, Jenny handles Nancy's travel, and often books her in a boutique hotel that caters to businesspeople. . . .

EXAMPLE 3: THE LATE-NIGHT ROOM SERVICE ATTENDANT AT A HOTEL

Carson is the lone room service attendant during the graveyard shift at a boutique hotel that caters to business travelers. He reports to the daytime restaurant manager, whom he rarely sees, as well as having a dotted-line relationship with the night manager. Carson's job responsibilities include taking orders, preparing food, and delivering it to guests between midnight and six o'clock in the morning. Additionally, he assists the night manager with various clerical tasks and provides limited security and maintenance during late-night hours.

Anonymity

This is a good candidate for being a factor in Carson's lack of job fulfillment, as he has little regular contact with other employees. That is why the daytime restaurant manager will have to go out of his way to get to know Carson, and will need to use alternate means of communication to stay in touch with him over time. He'll also have to work with the night manager to ensure that she develops rapport with Carson and gives him a sense of belonging.

Irrelevance

This is another likely cause of job dissatisfaction. Carson's manager will need to help him understand that on the rare occasions when guests require his services, they will almost always be in a position of unusual, even serious need. In many cases, those guests will have arrived late due to a flight delay or a red-eye trip, or they will be unable to sleep or even feeling ill. The room service attendant will be in a unique position to make a meaningful and lasting impact on that guest's comfort, even more than his colleagues on the day shift.

In addition to the impact that Carson has on guests, he also can make a meaningful difference in the day-to-day life of the night manager, both by providing clerical assistance and by being a source of good company during a potentially lonely time.

Immeasurement

Though Carson may well receive tips and compliments from guests, better measurements are available to his manager. That's not to say he shouldn't track the number of comments submitted by guests who receive exemplary service from Carson. But he could also have Carson measure other things, like the time it takes to turn around orders and requests from guests. He should also check in with the night manager, who is one of Carson's internal customers, about the quality of his work.

By the way, on Saturday mornings when Carson gets off work, he usually does his grocery shopping. . . .

EXAMPLE 4: THE BOX BOY AT THE GROCERY STORE

Andy is a sixteen-year-old high school student who works at the supermarket on weekends, bagging groceries and helping customers get them to their cars. He reports to the manager of cashiers.

Anonymity

Andy knows that he's somewhere near the bottom of the food chain at the grocery store. Though he has a pretty good relationship with a few of the cashiers, he probably feels like he's not high on the boss's list of priorities. The manager needs to find a way to connect with Andy around something that matters to him. Like football. An occasional conversation about the San Francisco 49ers— or a free football magazine from the newspaper rack—might be a good first step. Eventually, he'll want to develop a more substantive and authentic relationship that will make Andy feel more committed to the store and more enthusiastic about going above and beyond in his job.

Irrelevance

It would be easy for Andy to decide that his job was menial and unimportant, just a way to earn extra money on weekends. His manager needs to help him figure out how to make a difference in the lives of his customers, and perhaps even in the lives of the cashiers. Andy could consider doing something unique to make the check-out experience more fun for customers. That might include giving them a weather report or sports scores, asking a trivia question, or having an inspiring quote for them. Again, if this sounds silly, consider whether it would make the shopping experience better for customers, and the working experience better for Andy. Great managers, and companies, don't let the initial appearance of silliness prevent them from doing what is ultimately meaningful and differentiating.

Immeasurement

This is a challenge in many service jobs like Andy's. What his manager needs to do is help Andy establish a few ways to gauge his day-to-day success. Maybe it's the number of times he makes a customer laugh. Or maybe even the cashiers. Or perhaps it is about reducing the amount of time that customers have to wait before their groceries are ready to go. Or the time it takes him to move customers through the line. Whatever measurement is used, it's important that Andy be able to monitor his own success, and that when he leaves his shift, he knows how he performed that day.

By the way, did I mention that Andy likes football?

EXAMPLE 5: THE WIDE RECEIVER

Michael is the recently acquired star wide receiver for the local professional team. He is twenty-five years old, makes $4.2 million a year, lives in a beautiful home, travels to games in chartered jets, and stays in five-star hotels.

Anonymity

People will be surprised to learn that Michael—like many athletes in his bracket—is miserable in his job. They'll be even more surprised to learn that anonymity is a big part of it. Though Michael is famous and receives attention and adulation from fans and the media alike, he doesn't feel his coach knows or cares about him beyond the football field. When Michael moved to the area after being traded, the coach didn't ask him about his personal life or his transition to a new town. That coach needs to talk to Michael about more than his injuries and his statistics. He needs to understand what Michael's interests are off the field, and what he might want to do when his football career is over. Otherwise, Michael is going to feel like a commodity. A precious one, sure, but a commodity nonetheless.

Irrelevance

Many professional athletes like Michael either lose sight of, or never develop, a sense of how they make a difference in the lives of others. They see themselves as merely playing a game, one with no impact on real life. Michael's coach needs to help him understand that by playing well, he actually makes people happy. There are fans who spend a considerable amount of their disposable income on tickets so they can watch their team, and when that team wins, they are more likely to have a good week. As crazy as that may seem to some people, it's a reality and provides an incentive for Michael to play his best.

And Michael needs to realize that when he plays with determination and competitiveness and sportsmanship—and takes the time to sign an autograph and demonstrate genuine appreciation to fans—those fans are more likely to feel proud of themselves and their community.

Beyond the fans, Michael can also influence the people who work for the team. Everyone from the general manager to the head coach to the equipment assistant to the team receptionist will have greater job security and a sense of accomplishment if their team wins. That impacts their spouses and children in nontrivial ways. If Michael doesn't realize the effect he has on the lives of fans and team employees, he and the team are losing out on a powerful source of motivation.

Immeasurement

This is one area that Michael will probably not be lacking greatly, as wins and losses are a pretty good indicator of success on the field. However, Michael doesn't control the outcome of a game or season, and he will need to look at other measurables for his performance and behavior. Off the field, fan-related events and interaction with employees in the organization might be something he wants to monitor on a regular basis. Whatever the case, Michael needs some way of measuring how he is impacting the people that make his job relevant.

By the way, Michael is remodeling his home. . . .

EXAMPLE 6: THE CONSTRUCTION FOREMAN

Peter is one of three foremen at a residential construction firm. He has seventeen employees working on three different crews, building and remodeling high-quality homes. Peter is extremely fulfilled in his work.

Anonymity

This is not a problem for Peter as he has worked at the company for twenty-two years and has a close personal relationship with his boss and colleagues, all of whom he regards as friends. They know Peter and his wife well, and are both interested and involved in his pursuits outside of work.

Irrelevance

Peter's job satisfaction wasn't always high. After a number of years on the job, he began to lose some of his passion for the work he loved when he realized that many of his customers, some of whom were extremely wealthy, didn't fully appreciate what they were getting. His boss had to remind him, again and again at first, that beyond the actual work he was overseeing, he was impacting the lives of the people he managed. Many of those people had not finished high school, or had immigrated to the United States to give their kids a better future, and Peter was going to be one of the most important people to help them in that pursuit. Eventually, Peter came to see that his role as manager and mentor was more meaningful than what he did as a project manager, though the two were inextricably connected.

Immeasurement

Measuring success is not much of an issue for Peter either. Budgets and time lines have always been good metrics, and customers are usually quick to provide information about their levels of satisfaction (though dissatisfaction provokes even quicker input). As for measuring his impact on employees, Peter prides himself on his ability to retain his people, and to watch them buy homes, send their kids to college, and save money for their future. He also has found it immensely gratifying that they seemed to enjoy coming to work.

By the way, Peter's daughter Nancy is vice president of marketing at a medium-sized software company. . . .

TAKING ACTION

So how can you go about putting all this into action? The answer depends on who you are.

If you're a manager . . .

Try taking three simple steps to make your employees less miserable and more fulfilled. The first of those is an honest *self-assessment,* asking a few obvious questions related to each of the three signs.

Anonymity: "Do I really know my people? Their interests? How they spend their spare time? Where they are in their lives?"

Irrelevance: "Do they know who their work impacts, and how?"

Immeasurement: "Do they know how to assess their own progress or success?"

Next, consider doing *employee assessments,* allowing people to provide information that will either confirm or deny the accuracy of the answers in each of the three areas.

Finally, develop a plan to shore up any inadequacies around the three signs. That could mean a series of simple one-on-one meetings, or even a team session like the one in the fable.

And rather than being ambiguous or vague, which runs the risk of making employees suspect an ulterior motive, it's a good idea to just explain the three signs and what you are trying to do.

If you're an employee, job hunter, or recent college grad...

You can do some things to increase the odds that your job will be fulfilling. First, talk to your boss (or prospective boss) about the three signs of a miserable job, and your desire to avoid them. Most people really do want to be good managers, and if they know that they can become good at relatively low cost, they'll often be willing to change their behavior.

But you can't be afraid to talk to them about it. "Hey, I just read a book about how to make a job fulfilling, and I want to tell you about it. Not that you're a bad boss. It's just that I think I would do a better job and like working here even more if I were able to get a few things from you."

Explain that you want them to know who you are and what your interests and aspirations are, how your job impacts someone else, and how you can better measure your success or progress. If your manager isn't interested in providing those things, you can smile nicely and say it's not a problem, and then go dust off your résumé and start looking for a non-miserable job.

If you're looking for a great job, ask the hiring managers who interview you if they typically take an interest in employees, how the job they're discussing has an impact on people inside or outside the firm, and how you will be measured. If you're hearing answers that indicate anonymity, irrelevance, or immeasurement, know that the chances of job fulfillment are apt to be low.

If you're an executive, HR professional, or consultant and you're interested in establishing an organization-wide program around improving employee fulfillment . . .
Try a short, practical training session. This would involve teaching managers about the three signs, and then helping them put together plans for addressing them with their respective employees.

For products, downloadable tools, and other advice about implementing any of these suggestions, go to www.miserablejob.com.

THE MINISTRY
OF MANAGEMENT

I have always thought it was a shame that more people don't go into "giving" professions. In fact, I have occasionally felt pangs of guilt that I didn't choose a career that was completely focused on serving others. I have deep admiration for dedicated and hard-working clergy, social workers, or missionaries, and I wonder why I haven't abandoned my career and moved into one of those kinds of jobs.

While I have not completely abandoned the idea of one day doing that, I have come to the realization that all managers can—and really should—view their work as a ministry. A service to others.

By helping people find fulfillment in their work, and helping them succeed in whatever they're doing, a manager can have a profound impact on the emotional, financial, physical, and spiritual health of workers and their families. They can also create an environment where employees do the same for their peers, giving them a sort of ministry of their own. All of which is nothing short of a gift from God.

And so I suppose that the real shame is not that more people aren't working in positions of service to others, but that so many managers haven't yet realized that they already are.

ACKNOWLEDGMENTS

As always, there are many people to acknowledge for their help with this book.

Thank you, Laura, for your confidence, and for letting me steal away to the hotel for writing time. And to my boys, thanks for understanding why Dad has to leave late at night, and for coming to keep me company from time to time.

Thanks to my colleagues at The Table Group. Tracy, for your dutiful and persistent guidance, and your personal and professional dedication to this book. Karen, for listening to my ramblings in the Oklahoma City airport that day when the idea for this book came to me. To Amy, Jeff, Michele, Lynne, and Alison, for making my job anything but miserable. I am blessed to count you all as friends.

Special thanks to my mom and dad, and my brother and sister, for being so supportive and interested in my work, both now and throughout my life. Dad, for sharing your opinions about your occasionally miserable job with me, and for enduring it so I could go to college. And Mom, for your encouragement, and for always listening and helping Dad deal with his work. Vince, thanks for sharing a few miserable jobs with me during our youth. And Ritamarie, for the special work you do with me now.

Thanks to all the employees who were part of my work-related education over the years, from Maitia's Basque Restaurant and California Republic Bank in Bakersfield, California, to Bain & Company and Oracle and Sybase in the San Francisco Bay Area. From the dishwashers and waitresses and tellers to the consultants and executives, you all contributed to my understanding of and passion for finding fulfillment at work.

And I'm grateful to the many managers I had in those jobs: Frank Sr., Frank Jr., Annie, Frank, Steve, Cindy, Brenda, Rena, Torrey, David, Giffin, John, Anne, Jay, Greg, Meg, Rob, Noosheen, Gary, Mike, Nancy, Sally, Mike, Mark, Janet, and Mitchell, and anyone I might have forgotten.

Thanks to the folks at Jossey-Bass/Wiley, for your enthusiasm and commitment. Thank you Susan, Rebecca, Deborah, Cedric, Carolyn, Erik, Rob, Larry, Dean, Stephen, and the many, many others spread around the country who make it possible for my books to come about and find their way to the market.

And I'm always thankful to Jim Levine and all the folks at Levine Greenberg who represent me. Jim, your steady and genuine interest in The Table Group makes such a difference to us, and never ceases to amaze us.

Thanks to the friends and family who gave us feedback and ideas and support relating to this book, especially Al and Patty. Thanks to Greg for making it possible for Tracy to work evenings from time to time to get this book across the finish line. And thanks to Matthew and Tom and Daniel for giving so much of your time and advice without counting the cost.

And to my other guy friends—Andy, Barry, Brian, Dante, Eric, Jamie, John, Rob, and Will—for your interest in my work, which means more to me than you know.

Finally, I thank God for the gift of work, and for allowing me to do what I love in a way that serves You.

ABOUT THE AUTHOR

Patrick Lencioni is founder and president of The Table Group, a management consulting firm specializing in executive team development and organizational health. As a consultant and keynote speaker, he has worked with thousands of senior executives in organizations ranging from Fortune 500s and high-tech start-ups to universities and nonprofits. Clients who have engaged his services include Southwest Airlines, Sam's Club, Microsoft, New York Life, Cox Communications, Washington Mutual, Visa, FedEx, and the U.S. Military Academy, West Point, to name a few. He is the author of six nationally recognized books, including the *New York Times* best-seller *The Five Dysfunctions of a Team* (Jossey-Bass, 2002).

Patrick lives in the San Francisco Bay Area with his wife, Laura, and their four sons, Matthew, Connor, Casey, and Michael.

To learn more about Patrick and The Table Group, please visit www.tablegroup.com.

the table group
a patrick lencioni company

The Table Group is dedicated to helping organizations of all kinds function more effectively through better leadership, teamwork, and overall health.

Visit our website, and explore:

Irrelevance

Immeasurement

JOB
MISERY

Anonymity

The Three Signs of a Miserable Job

For Miserable Job tools, downloads, and products
go directly to **www.miserablejob.com**

For information about Lencioni's other books and
The Table Group's products and services, please visit

www.tablegroup.com 925.299.9700